I Know What You're Thinking

Using the Four Codes of Reading
People to Improve Your Life

Lillian Glass, Ph.D.

John Wiley & Sons, Inc.

Published by John Wiley & Sons, Inc.
Published simultaneously in Canada

This publication is designed to provide accurate and authoritative information in regard to the subject matter covered. It is sold with the understanding that the publisher is not engaged in rendering professional services. If professional advice or other expert assistance is required, the services of a competent professional person should be sought.

ISBN 0-471-38140-3

Printed in the United States of America

10 9 8 7 6 5 4 3 2 1

I am dedicating this book to my late father, Abraham Glass,
and my late brother, Manny M. Glass. These wonderful, brilliant men
were truly masters in the art of reading people. May their wisdom I now
share with you enrich your life as it has mine; may their insights give
you as sharp an understanding of others as they gave me.

Contents

Acknowledgments

First, I would like to acknowledge my lovely mother, Rosalie Glass, who is as beautiful on the inside as she is on the outside. I thank her for teaching me how to be a good observer. I am also grateful for her kind and caring words and her constant encouragement throughout the course of this book as well as throughout my life. I am truly blessed.

To Lambear, my Lhasa Apso, for his frequent visits so I could take a cuddle break. I thank him for making me smile and providing insight and practical experience into how animals communicate and how they read others.

To Tom Miller, my editor, for allowing me to share this book with others.

To Marshall Klein, for his support and belief in me.

To Marc Chamlin, my entertainment attorney, for always watching out for me.

To the late, great Dr. Paul Cantalupo, who was one of my closest friends and largely responsible for my obtaining a Ph.D. in the field of counseling psychology. I thank him for his recognition of my talents, for his incredible support and wisdom, and for the long hours we spent discussing this exciting topic. Our friendship will never be forgotten and will forever be cherished.

And to all the wonderful people I have met throughout my life who have touched me and believed in me, I thank you from the bottom of my heart. I can't begin to express how much your support and kind words have meant to me.

PART ONE

The Art and Science of Reading People

Introduction

When I was a little girl growing up in Miami, my late father, Abraham Glass, and I used to play a game. Little did I know this game would be the key to my professional success. He would take me to the movies and at the beginning of the film, there was always a newsreel and a cartoon. After the movie, as we walked down the street to Royal Castle to eat some hamburgers and drink a birch beer from a frozen mug, my father would ask a question, such as what was the name of the dog in the cartoon. If I could tell him, he would buy me a present.

When I was with him, I learned to be extra aware of my surroundings, conscious of everyone I met and every place I went. There was no room for zoning out, because a potential gift was on the line.

My father would usually ask me to recall details like, "What color was the lady's dress? Why was that person sad? Who did that man (or lady) remind you of?" He was constantly prodding me to be aware of the world around me, forcing me to observe the tiniest detail. Wherever we went, he would point things out: the colors on a small bird's beak, a change in the direction of the wind before a tropical storm, the smell of a freshly mowed lawn, the taste of a succulent ripe mango. His gift was to teach me to heighten all my senses and be totally aware of life around me.

From an early age, I was primed for what would eventually become my life's work. I was so fascinated by this study that I learned as much as I could throughout my formal education. My father prepared me to do well as a student, leading to me to two Ph.D.s, one in counseling psychology, the other in communication disorders. During my education, I learned what was required to help people with every aspect of improved communication skills.

Analyzing speech and voice qualities can provide keen insight into a person's mental health. The rate of a person's voice, pitch, loudness, voice quality, stridency; how much or even how little the person says, all may serve as an accurate barometer to determining the individual's emotional status and, in turn, personality characteristics.

The work of numerous anthropologists, including the popular research done by Desmond Morris and others, have provided the essentials of understanding human facial expression in order to better understand human communication. This information gives us a greater understanding about people's behavior, which gives us a deeper insight into their character. Likewise, the literature concerning body language and how people comport themselves offers an entirely different avenue of understanding from simply listening to their words.

When a person is analyzed on a consistent basis over time in terms of all four modalities—body, face, voice, and speaking patterns—others can accurately decipher which personality types are best and least suited for the person. By observing the true essence of people through these four modalities of communication, we are better able to perceive ourselves and determine which people we should embrace or reject to improve our quality of life.

———

The technology in this book is based on more than two decades of empirical data collected from thousands of clients whose communication skills I was able to help enhance. They come from various walks of life and all age groups, including some who were psychologically or emotionally troubled and some who were disabled. There were also those who were extremely gifted, mentally healthy and well-balanced individuals, among them athletes, physicians, therapists, homemakers, business people, attorneys, and politicians. I have also worked with high-profile entertainers, including Dustin Hoffman, Julio Iglesias, Andy Garcia, Dolly Parton, Ben Vereen, Nicolas Cage, Sean Connery, Keanu Reeves, Rene Russo, Melanie Griffith, and Marlee Matlin.

My clients have learned how to communicate more effectively, improve their public presentations, enhance vocal quality, rectify poor speaking patterns, learn an accent, modify a dialect, and develop greater self-confidence. They have become better communicators in both their business and their personal relationships.

As I worked with people in Beverly Hills and New York City, I scrutinized not only the way they spoke, but their entire persona. Evaluating them from head to toe, developing a diagnosis and plan of attack, I examined every glitch in their speech, the way they held their heads, their facial expressions, eye contact, the way in which they walked, sat, or stood. I carefully listened to and analyzed every detail of what they said and how they said it.

I observed my clients' facial and body movements, their posture and how they comported themselves. I noticed that certain combinations of these vocal, speech, body, and facial language components were consistent with certain personality types. Patterns emerged, and I was able to distinguish fourteen personality profiles.

My awareness of my clients' outer beings gave me insight into their inner beings so much so that many of them began to think I was psychic. How else could I know so much about what they were feeling or what was haunting them psychologically, even though they weren't verbalizing what was bothering them?

By analyzing their external demeanor and how they spoke, I was able to assess their personality and make an accurate judgment about what was going on inside of them. Just as the content of what someone says and the way it is said reveals the truth, *the body and the face don't lie.* I could tell what was going on with my clients psychologically, merely by listening and observing. I could tell volumes by the way they stood or the way they looked at me.

My clients were routinely astounded by the revelations that emerged during our sessions. One such client, Dan, a forty-eight-year-old, highly successful businessman, was beside himself when I told him I felt he was probably abused by his father when he was younger because he was full of rage. Dan couldn't believe I knew this secret since he had told no one. But I found it readily apparent as I consistently observed his tense jaw, hard glottal attacking tones, and twitches and physical nuances whenever he referred to his father. This process of microscopically examining Dan's outside behavior allowed me to tune into his inside behavior.

The power of this technique has enabled me to look into a person's character and personality—to foresee what would happen in the future. I was able to assess personality and provide clients with a prescription for what was required in order to improve their behavior so they would not be stuck in situations that were not in their best interests.

Ted, a thirty-seven-year-old restaurant manager, constantly mumbled and his voice tended to fade at the end of sentences. He had a high-pitched voice for his husky 6-foot-2 frame and looked down at his shoes when he was asked a question. When asked about his family, he avoided eye contact, hunched over, bowed his head and could barely be heard.

I asked him how long it had been since he had seen his children. He immediately broke down and tearfully told me he hadn't known their whereabouts for years. I told him his first priority was to hire a private investigator to help find his children since that was the real reason he had trouble speaking. He needed to act like a responsible man to sound like a responsible man.

Ted's speaking pattern and body movements reflected his insecurity, lack of self-worth, and the intense shame he felt for abandoning his children. Ultimately, Ted took my advice. He hired a private investigator who found his children and Ted renewed his close relationship with them.

Shortly after he was reunited with his loved ones, Ted's voice automatically dropped two octaves and resonated when he spoke. His voice no longer trailed off at the end of sentences. He didn't hang his head when he spoke. What I told him during our first session came true.

It was also rewarding to encourage celebrity clients before they emerged as stars. I sensed their winning potential based on how they scored verbally, vocally, and in their body and facial language.

Among them was actor Andy Garcia. I sensed he would be a major star the moment he walked into my office. He had a confident walk, a firm handshake, and great eye contact; he was poised, well spoken, elegant, determined, and focused. As they say in Hollywood, he had *it*. *It* is a winning quality that makes you want to pay attention when the person speaks. Charisma is what you say and how you say *it* and how you look when you say it all at once. Your body and facial language are in alignment and people like what they see and hear. *It* is a kind of electricity that opens doors because of how these people present themselves and how one feels in their presence. Throughout this book I will show you how to read people who have *it*.

A few years ago, I was asked by *Newsweek* to read what superstars such as Tina Turner, Helen Hunt, and Sharon Stone were really trying to say as they appeared on the covers of the nation's top magazines. Even though these women were positioned similarly, with their arms akimbo and hands on their hips, the messages they displayed through their photos were quite different. Sharon

Stone's message screamed, "I'm sexy, come get me," while Helen Hunt's message reflected a casual tone, "Hey, I'm one of you guys." Tina Turner's message declared female power.

In a piece I did for *Redbook*, I had to read photos of various celebrities and give feedback on the status of their relationships. One set of photographs was of Tom Hanks and his wife, Rita Wilson. They looked like they were having a great time as they gazed into each other's eyes with love and concern. They leaned into one another as though they were a real couple, which, of course, they were. They appeared to be appreciative of each other and this certainly is reflected by their marriage of close to fifteen years.

In *I Know What You're Thinking,* I will demonstrate how the power to know the truth is something that everyone can learn. It is not reserved for the privileged or for psychics or for those who are highly educated or intuitive. It is for everyone. I will share information about how to assess any situation accurately, which will enhance both your personal and your professional life.

I will allow you to determine how well you read others, then how well you read yourself. You will learn how to decipher each of the four codes of communication: the speech code, the voice code, the body code, and the facial code. You will learn exercises to help you better tap into your ability to read others. Then you will discover how to integrate each of these codes into a specific Personality Profile, making it easy for you to identify someone who possesses traits that affect you, positively or negatively.

This book can literally change your life as it embodies techniques my clients have used so well. Like them, it can help you become much more aware and secure so that you will not make as many mistakes in your judgment of others. It will help you think more clearly as you learn to trust your instincts and make better choices in your dealings with people, thereby enriching all aspects of your life.

CHAPTER 1

The "How Well Do I Read People?" Quiz

In order to assess your grasp of the essential communication skills it takes to discern the truth, you must first take a look at your current abilities.

This test will help you discover how you rank in knowing yourself and others. You may have the ability to read every nuance a person expresses. You may be able to use it to your advantage so you rarely make a mistake in judging others. You may or may not have the ability to confront a person whom you have read because you are afraid to rock the boat or make waves. You may believe it is more important for you to be liked than to have your integrity remain intact. You may be the type of person who can't read the cues, or you may be so out of it that you've become a walking target for bad relationships.

This quiz is specifically designed to discover if you are already a person who can read others and how well you can accomplish that task.

Answer each question by choosing "true" or "false." Respond honestly. The first thing that pops into your mind is usually the right answer, so don't second-guess yourself.

1. Every time I walk out of the house, I am completely aware of people who are around me.
   TRUE_____ FALSE___✓___

2. When I am walking on the street I always know if there are people walking in back of me or to the sides of me.
   TRUE_____ FALSE___✓___

3. The first thing I notice about a person is the face.
   TRUE___✓___ FALSE_____

4. I always notice what a person is wearing.
   TRUE___✓___ FALSE_____

5. I always ask myself why I don't feel good about a person or a situation.
   TRUE_____ FALSE___✓___

6. I immediately observe something about someone's behavior that I don't like and will form an opinion about that person.
   TRUE___✓___ FALSE_____

7. I am not surprised when my initial impression is correct.
   TRUE___✗___ FALSE___✓___

8. If I don't like someone, I never ignore how I really feel about the person.
   TRUE_____ FALSE___✓___

9. If I don't like someone I stop and analyze why that person rubs me the wrong way.
   TRUE___✓___ FALSE_____

10. If I like a person I often reflect on why I like that person.
    TRUE___✓___ FALSE_____

11. If I dislike someone I just met for no specific reason, I will not ignore those feelings or attribute them to just having a bad day.
    TRUE_____ FALSE___✓_____

12. I remember almost everything people say to me.
    TRUE_____ FALSE___✓_____

13. When talking to people I pay close attention to their facial expressions.
    TRUE___✓_____ FALSE_____

14. I listen carefully to people's tone, so I am always aware of how they are feeling when they speak to me.
    TRUE___✓_____ FALSE_____

15. I am not gullible; I don't believe everything people say to me.
    TRUE_____ FALSE___✓_____

16. I question people and make them accountable for what they say by asking them to explain themselves, especially if I don't agree with them.
    TRUE_____ FALSE___✓_____

17. I can usually tell if someone is lying to me or stretching the truth.
    TRUE___✓_____ FALSE_____

18. I can always tell when someone is angry.
    TRUE___✓_____ FALSE_____

19. I can always tell when someone is sad.
    TRUE_____ FALSE___✓_____

20. I can always tell when someone is afraid.
    TRUE_____ FALSE___✓_____

21. I can always tell when someone is mad at me.
    TRUE___✓_____ FALSE_____

22. I can always tell when someone loves me.
    TRUE_____ FALSE___✓_____

23. I can always tell when someone is happy.
    TRUE_____✓_____ FALSE_____

24. I can always tell when someone really doesn't like me.
    TRUE_____ FALSE_____✓_____

25. I can always tell when someone is surprised.
    TRUE____✓____ FALSE_____

26. I can always tell when someone is honest with me.
    TRUE_____ FALSE____✓____

27. I can always tell when someone is indifferent.
    TRUE_____ FALSE____✓____

28. I can tell when someone is bored by me while I speak to the person.
    TRUE____✓____ FALSE_____

29. I always know when I have worn out my welcome.
    TRUE____✓____ FALSE_____

30. I usually stay away from certain people who spell trouble for me.
    TRUE_____ FALSE_____✓_____

31. I usually remember how people stand, walk, or comport themselves in case I have to describe them to someone.
    TRUE_____ FALSE____✓____

32. I recall exactly how a person sounded when relating a specific story to me.
    TRUE____✓____ FALSE_____

33. I have little difficulty remembering incidents from the past and how I felt when I went through those experiences.
    TRUE____✓____ FALSE_____

34. I can easily recall the speaking pattern of a person I just met.
    TRUE_____ FALSE____✓____

35. If I had to describe the way someone spoke, I could easily recall it and describe it to other people.
TRUE_____ FALSE_____

36. Even though I was not specifically being threatened or challenged, I have felt afraid or uncomfortable around a person I just met.
TRUE__✓__ FALSE_____

37. When I am on vacation, I tend to notice things to which others seem oblivious.
TRUE__✓__ FALSE_____

38. I am often the first to locate something.
TRUE_____ FALSE__✓__

39. I am excellent at recalling exactly what someone has told me.
TRUE_____ FALSE__✓__

40. I usually remember how to get somewhere even though I may have been there only a few times.
TRUE_____ FALSE__✓__

41. It is easy for me to express my emotions.
TRUE_____ FALSE__✓__

42. I have no trouble letting people know I am angry.
TRUE_____ FALSE__✓__

43. It is easy for me to express love and affection.
TRUE_____ FALSE__✓__

44. I am in touch with all of my feelings.
TRUE_____ FALSE__✓__

45. I pay careful attention to the flavor, texture, and consistency of what I eat.
TRUE__✓__ FALSE_____

46. My ears perk up when somebody says something out of line.
TRUE__✓__ FALSE_____

47. I rarely ignore a backhanded compliment or cutting remark and immediately pick up on what the person is really trying to say.
TRUE_____ FALSE____✓____

48. When I am excited about something I often laugh out loud, dance with excitement, or let out a loud tone.
TRUE_____ FALSE____✓____

49. When something doesn't feel right to me, I quickly notice a physical reaction—a tightening sensation in my throat or the pit of my stomach.
TRUE___✓_____ FALSE_____

50. I tend to perspire a lot when something doesn't feel right to me or when I am under a lot of tension.
TRUE___✓_____ FALSE_____

51. I notice I tend to eat too much or too little when something is bothering me emotionally.
TRUE___✓_____ FALSE_____

52. Even though others are enthusiastic about something, I tend not to be influenced by peer pressure.
TRUE_____ FALSE___✓_____

53. I can always tell when I have upset someone.
TRUE___✓_____ FALSE_____

54. I can always tell when someone genuinely likes me.
TRUE_____ FALSE___✓____

55. I can describe a person's looks and appearance in great detail.
TRUE___✓_____ FALSE_____

56. If people are inconsistent in what they say, I will often bring it to their attention.
TRUE_____ FALSE___✓____

57. If I suspect someone is not telling the truth, I will continue questioning the person in detail.
TRUE___✓_____ FALSE_____

58. I always remember the first impression I had about a person.
    TRUE___✓___ FALSE_____
59. I can always tell what kind of a mood someone is in.
    TRUE_____ FALSE__✓____
60. I am fully aware of when someone says something that doesn't
    match facial expression or body language.
    TRUE___✓___ FALSE_____

Scoring the Quiz

Now that you have taken the quiz, give yourself one point for every
answer that you marked "true." Give yourself 0 points for each
answer you marked "false." Count the total number of points. 29

What Do Your Answers Mean?

Give yourself one point for each "true" answer, then see what this
score reveals about your people reading ability.

60 Points: You Are Totally Tuned In

If you answered "true" to every one of these questions, congratulations! This means you are completely tuned in and very much
aware of yourself. You are also aware of other people and the
world around you. You probably tend to make few mistakes in
terms of sizing up people. You usually appear to do the right thing.
Your moral and ethical values are intact and you truly care about
others.

You do not accept people at face value. Instead, you are an
accurate judge of them. You tend to be a sensitive and caring human

being with a tendency to look deeper and see people for who they really are. You tend to be an achiever, a leader. You have the potential to contribute meaningful things to society.

Even though you scored 100 percent, there is more work to be done. It is essential for you to further enhance and finely tune your keenly sensitive people reading skills.

40–59 Points: You Have Good Instincts

This score means you have good instincts when it comes to most things, but there are times when you feel like kicking yourself or tearing out your hair for not trusting your intuition. You tend to be a bit hard on yourself when you've done something knowing full well that the consequences would be bad. You are extremely critical of yourself. But for the most part you tend to have a good sense of self, and genuinely like yourself.

You need to have an even clearer sense of knowing you are much more often right than wrong. You need to further explore issues of self-esteem and self-confidence and work on leadership skills. Finally, you need to explore commitment issues. Work on changing your mind in various situations and try to abide by your first decisions.

Be certain that what you are doing in life pleases you first and everyone else second. You must closely examine what you want to do, not what you think you should do. Don't stifle your emotions. Go beneath the surface when you get to know people. Ask more pointed questions to discover who they really are and what they really think. Make a greater effort to get in touch with what is going on around you.

39–20 Points: You Play It Safe

You are the type of person who appreciates playing it safe and not making waves. You detest confrontation and love the status quo. It embarrasses you to ask people for things or to make yourself known to someone. You hate being conspicuous because it makes you feel self-conscious. You like to make everyone feel at ease. You would rather put people at ease and have yourself feel uncomfortable than have others feel uncomfortable. You cooperate and if something doesn't feel right, you usually ignore the feeling and do it anyway, much to your regret. However, you will most likely not say anything, but will keep it inside and suffer in silence.

Reading this book and absorbing its contents will undoubtedly change your life for the better. You will gain self-confidence and no one will be able to fool you. You will learn to trust yourself, which will allow you to know who else to trust. You will have a set of rules and guidelines from which you will not deviate, making you feel more secure and confident with others.

If you follow the advice on these pages, most people you already know will begin to notice just how much better you look and how you've changed. They will begin to see the new you emerge with increased self-esteem and self-confidence.

0–19 Points: You Need Help!

You need help desperately. You've probably made many mistakes in your life—way too many—because you have walked around wearing blinders. Unfortunately, this has made you an easy mark for others. You tend to be the kind of person who has a quiet and easygoing nature, one who takes a lot for granted. On the other hand, you could go to the other extreme—a person who makes plenty of noise and who's so self-absorbed you miss the signals of others.

If you are the type who makes these mistakes, your go-with-the-flow kind of sensibility makes you a better follower than a leader. Unfortunately, those you follow don't always lead you wisely. Most likely you have been ripped off and taken advantage of many times, but never tend to learn from your mistakes. You have come to believe that Murphy's Law—anything that can go wrong usually will—is a way of life for you.

If you are the talkative type, you are too busy making noise to pay attention so that you may accurately read others. That is why you seem to make all those awful mistakes.

You need to become more aware of the world around you and how you fit into it. You need to overhaul your belief systems as soon as possible, especially the way you see yourself and the world. You need to stop being so self-absorbed and to get your head out of the clouds; instead, get to know the people along the highway of life. Reading this book should be a priority in your life. In doing so, you can save a lot of grief and dramatically change your life so that Murphy's Law will never be the law of your land.

CHAPTER 2

Why It's So Important to Read People

Each of us has an innate ability to detect the truth in others and be in tune with circumstances and the world around us. Some of us are willing to face reading others head-on, while others are more apt to look the other way. Not everyone approaches the issue the same way. It's human nature.

- He makes me sick!
- I just adore her!
- I trusted him the minute I laid eyes on him!
- I just knew she was going to be a real bitch!
- Why didn't I go with my gut?
- I knew he was nothing but a liar!
- It was love at first sight!
- I knew she was going to be trouble!
- I knew he was going to cost me money in the long run!
- I could just kick myself! Why didn't I trust my instincts?

You *read* people every day without even realizing it. You make assessments as to whether a person is good or bad for you, honest or dishonest, if he or she should be in your life. In essence, you know right from wrong. Reading a person comes naturally. The problem is that most of us don't know how to translate what's behind that feeling and use the information to empower ourselves in a particular situation. In this chapter I'll show examples of specific situations that illustrate how reading people or not reading people affects your life.

We all fall into different categories. To find out kind of person you are, answer these questions.

1. Are you a decisive decision maker?
   a. Are you a doer and a leader with a strong sense of self, with strong moral values? No
   b. Do you know what you are doing and where you are going at all times? No
   c. Are you hardly ever wrong and do you usually make the right choices? No
   d. Are you tuned in when something doesn't feel right? Yes
2. Do you have good instincts most of the time? Yes
   a. Do you ever feel like kicking yourself for not trusting your instincts? Yes
   b. Do you usually make the right decisions? No
   c. Are you sometimes swayed by what others think? Yes
   d. Do you listen to others just to appease or please them? Yes
3. Are you someone who doesn't like to make waves? Yes
   a. Do you tend to ignore things when they don't seem right? Yes
   b. Do you hope things will work out on their own? sometimes
   c. Are you often confused about who to trust? Yes
   d. Do you often doubt yourself? Yes
4. Are you the kind of person who is constantly getting ripped off? Yes
   a. Have you often been tricked by people in business? Yes

b. Do you feel there are a lot of people who have done you wrong in your personal life? Yes
c. Does your refrain always seem to be "Why me?" or "It could only happen to me"? Yes
d. Do you believe most of what you read and most of what people tell you? Yes

Your Answers Reflect You

If you answered yes to all of the questions in Scenario One, you are a decisive leader. If you answered yes to only one or two, you are an indecisive leader.

In Scenario Two, if you answered yes to all four questions, you have great instincts. If you answered yes to only one or two, your instincts leave a lot to be desired.

In Scenario Three, if you answered no to all four questions, you are highly aware and don't have your head in the sand. If you answered yes to two or more, you need a lot of work in paying attention to what is going on around you.

In Scenario Four, if you answered no to all four questions, you are not a victim and you know what kind of people you are dealing with. If you answered yes to two or more, you had better open your eyes and start taking responsibility for your choices.

No More Victimization

How much money or time have you wasted because you chose the wrong person to work for you? A typical scenario is the contractor who assures you the work will only cost so much, then hits you with a bill that's double the estimate.

What about the job applicant who hands you the most dazzling resume you've ever seen but turns out to be a sloppy, unmotivated goof-off whose aim is to take advantage of the system at every turn. You feel emotionally and financially betrayed because this was not the person he or she seemed to be.

Wouldn't it be wonderful if we had a method that would allow us to predict accurately how we would get along based upon the way a person spoke, what he or she said, his or her body and facial language? Wouldn't it be great to know if someone was passive-aggressive or lying when declaring that he or she really loved you?

When your date tells you, "I had a great time. Let's go out again sometime next week," wouldn't you like to know if this was genuine, instead of just anxiously waiting for the phone to ring? Wouldn't you want to know if someone was cheating on you?

Why do we often ignore that inner voice that screams, or that twinge kicking in our tummy? Why do most of us refuse to recognize the signals? Why don't we want to hear even though it is blaring at us to stop and take heed? It is because most us of don't trust that what we are hearing or feeling is the truth. We don't trust that what we sense is right. Don't forget, our body doesn't lie.

We don't trust that sinking feeling in the pit of our stomach as being valid, telling us others may be bad for us. We do not embrace the idea that we may be involved in a situation that can potentially do us harm. To complicate matters, this decision to trust our feelings has to be made immediately—within seconds—or it may be too late. That's why so many of us make the same mistakes time and again: choosing the wrong people, getting involved in the wrong relationships, and finding the wrong business partners.

Reading People Can Save Your Life

Although child molesters, serial killers, rapists, and other criminals don't wear neon signs, their victims often say the perpetrators behaved in unusual ways. Whether it was a signal given through their body language, the way they looked at their potential victim, or their tone of voice, a feeling of danger was present. Listening and reacting to those feelings can save your life and the lives of loved ones.

Linda, a twenty-year-old college student, saw a young man heading toward her as she walked from her dormitory and immediately felt uneasy. He tried to stop her and asked for the correct time. She ignored him and hurriedly ran into the library, while noticing a sick feeling in the pit of her stomach. She thought nothing more about it until she was getting ready to leave the library. She asked three other students if she could walk with them to the dorm.

Listening to her instincts may have saved her life. The next morning, she saw a newspaper photo of the man who had given her the creeps the day before. This was the same man from whom she had run on her way to the library. He had raped several students before being apprehended that night.

Reading the Con Artist

Bonnie, a thirty-two-year-old teacher, met Devon, a thirty-eight-year-old, 6-foot-2-inch, handsome electrical contractor. He was romantic and he seemed too good to be true. The fact he was a little low on money and the fact she had to pay for all their dates didn't bother her, because he kept saying his paycheck was coming from Canada and would arrive any day. Any day turned into weeks and months. Still, he treated her like a queen.

Dates were on weekdays because he told her he had a job that required him to work weekends. Of course she couldn't call him there or he'd get fired. She only had his cell phone number. He said his house was under construction and it was a huge home. The two of them would live in this palace but she could not see it until it was completed.

Because she was a woman head over heels in love, she didn't notice his eye twitches, his blinking, his avoiding eye contact, and his shoulders rising as he offered excuse after excuse. She didn't listen to his high-pitched voice trailing off at the end of phrases or his "ers" and "ahs" whenever she questioned him in detail.

This scoundrel was a married man who had found a sucker to play with. And he took full advantage of her financially, sexually, and emotionally.

A Terrible Job Interview

Nina, a gregarious forty-six-year-old with the gift of gab, was in tears as she told me a story about a very important career opportunity that she blew. "I couldn't believe what happened," she explained. "I became mute during my meeting with this executive. I literally couldn't speak. This had never happened before. I could barely say my name and couldn't pitch my project to him. I literally went blank, stammered and stuttered and could not recover. I finally handed him my proposal. I was so embarrassed. Needless to say, the meeting soon ended and I didn't get the job."

As we discussed what happened during the meeting, it wasn't surprising why she froze. He gave her nothing! From the moment Nina walked in the office, he simply ignored her. He continued speaking on the phone and let Nina stand until he finished his conversation.

He never made eye contact, nor did he acknowledge that anyone was in the room or motion for her to be seated. When she tried small talk, he ignored her. He had casually said there would be two other people joining them, which further unsettled Nina.

He knew nothing about her background even though she had sent her resume several times. When she said she had two projects to pitch, he replied, without looking at her, "Only pitch one," delivered in a harsh, clipped monotone.

No wonder Nina's muscles tensed so much that her vocal muscles prevented her from speaking to this rude, inattentive person. It was a losing battle. Her mind knew it, and her body automatically responded. She wasn't going to get the project anyway, so why bother? After I explained why she shut down, Nina stopped crying and began to laugh. "My body was telling me to shut up and not deal with this jerk." How right she was!

The Date from Hell

Annette knew that something was not right with Chuck, but she went out with him anyway even though her gut screamed, "Don't go." She knew she shouldn't be going back to his dorm room, but she went anyway. She wanted to be polite. This politeness led to date rape.

"I felt ugly and ashamed," she said. "I sensed trouble right away. Chuck's language was so vulgar and filled with double entendres, some subtle and some not so subtle. He looked at me like I was an object. I should have known better than to be with him in the first place."

Annette is not at fault for being date raped, nor should she blame herself. Her saying no to Chuck should have been sufficient. But she needed to learn the skills of reading people.

An Undeserved Lawsuit

Mr. Jones knows what it's like to be financially and emotionally betrayed. Case in point: his nightmare employee, Patty. She was cute and charming and he liked her beautiful smile, but today he regrets not listening to her speech and voice codes—what she said and how she said it.

Unfortunately, Mr. Jones ignored what she was telling him. Had he listened more carefully, he would have seen that Patty was nothing but trouble. For one thing, she never stopped talking and was extremely narcissistic. She was usually the main topic of conversation, which usually centered on the same theme: how she was victimized by previous coworkers or bosses. Of course, they were jealous of her and her good looks.

Mr. Jones could not get past her seductive smile with the protruding lower lip, the flirtatious way she threw her shoulders back when she laughed, and the eyes that gazed upward as her head remained in a downward position. If he'd paid close attention, he would have realized that this was an overly dramatic, troubled woman full of woe who might as well have been talking to a therapist than a prospective employer.

But he didn't look or listen and as a result he suffered dire consequences She couldn't get along with her coworkers. Ultimately, she slapped the company with a huge sexual harassment suit. Mr. Jones learned the hard way that what you see and hear are what you get.

Cheated Lover

Bart was a wealthy, fifty-four-year-old entrepreneur with a problem. He was heartbroken about a woman he believed was jilting him.

"She's visiting her sister in Texas for a month and I'm only allowed to call her during the day. Apparently, her sister comes home early from work, goes to bed early, and doesn't want the phone disturbing her," Bart explained.

"She says she loves me but she's not willing to make a commitment. I have done so much for her and she doesn't appreciate it. I buy her great gifts and she seems to take it for granted. When I call her, she always says she'll call me back and never does. Two days ago, she left a message on my machine saying she would be in Texas two more weeks because her sister needed her there. She always seems to be on the go whenever I talk to her, running out like she has no time for me. I'm beginning to think there is someone else in the picture."

Bart was right. He finally was able to catch the lady in a lie. She tearfully admitted she had, indeed, found another man.

Although he was heartbroken, Bart was at least relieved to

know his gut sense had been right. Her deeds spoke louder than the empty "I love yous" he heard from her lips.

Marriage Mistakes

While it is not uncommon for people who are about to marry to have pre-wedding jitters, they should think twice about taking the plunge if the misgivings don't subside.

I will never forget counseling Jim, a thirty-nine-year-old CPA, on his marital problems, only to hear him say, "I absolutely knew I was making the biggest mistake of my life on my wedding day. I knew it when I was walking down the aisle. In fact, tears began to roll down my cheeks as I stood there, about to repeat my vows. These were not tears of joy. They were tears of fear—knowing it was wrong. I went through with the ceremony and have lived to regret it each day," said Jim.

"If you felt that way, why didn't you call off the wedding?" I asked.

"From the time we were first dating we always seemed to bicker with each other about the smallest things," Jim responded. "She always had to be right and so did I. She was always trying to change me—my clothes, my hair, my manners. This happened more and more as it got closer to the wedding date.

"When I stood at the altar all I could recall was our constant bickering. I was hoping I would get past the resentment and anger toward her. I tried to block it out, thinking it was just a case of pre-wedding nerves. But it wasn't. After we were married, our bickering got worse and she seemed to criticize everything I did."

Had Jim been able to verbalize his concerns to his bride-to-be and undergo some premarital therapy or made the decision to not go through with the wedding, he would have saved himself a lot of fighting, heartache, legal bills, and money problems as a result of the divorce he went through.

Business Blunders

If you make a mistake in hiring, the cost of replacing that employee is usually two and a half times the person's annual salary. If you hire someone at $30,000 a year it will cost you $75,000 should you choose to replace him or her—not to mention the emotional costs.

Theresa was recommended for a job by Mark's best friend, Gabriel. Gabriel said Theresa knew her stuff and would be a great asset to his company. But Mark didn't like her aggressive tone and the hostile way she answered questions. Because he found her to be rather unpleasant and didn't like being in her presence, Mark hurried through the interview. When she left the room, he felt a sense of relief. When he spoke to Gabriel later that day, he asked, "Is Theresa always that intense?"

Gabriel laughed and repeated that she "knew her stuff." He called to offer her the job, which proved to be one of the biggest mistakes of his career. Not only was Theresa hostile and disrespectful, she questioned his every request. She had a difficult time with other employees and affected the morale of the department. People seemed tense and complained about her. Customers found her rude and impossible to be around and sales ultimately dwindled.

By not paying attention to his feelings about Theresa based upon their first meeting, Mark's decision to hire her cost the company financial losses and a dip in morale.

Two Scenarios: Positive and Negative

Love at First Sight

You can probably relate to the following scenario, which took place at a cocktail party attended by my client Steven, a successful businessman. Even though he was looking forward to the event, he was exhausted from a long day's work and just wanted to go home. As he looked around, searching for one of his associates, something happened that changed everything about the evening.

He noticed a gorgeous woman standing at a table across the room. He was compelled to walk over and speak to her. As he drew closer, he liked what he saw—how she stood and the way she moved.

He introduced himself and broke the ice with a humorous comment and a compliment, and she responded with a teasing comeback. He was even more intrigued by the sound of her voice, and the way her upper lip curled when she spoke. He found himself standing closer to her, continuously smiling as he kept gazing directly at her face.

At this point, he couldn't care less if a bomb went off outside. He just couldn't take his eyes off her. All he wanted was to be in her presence and absorb everything about her. Suddenly, he noticed he had difficulty catching his breath.

His heart was beating a mile a minute and his throat seemed to close off so he couldn't swallow. After what seemed to be an eternity, he mustered enough courage to ask the mystery lady for her card, which she gladly handed to him. He called her and the two of them began to date until six months ago, when they finally married.

Notice the intense positive draw Steven felt—his initial reaction, his instinct to walk over and speak to the woman, and what happened when he was in her presence. He changed *physically*. His breathing was labored. His skin tingled, his heart beat faster, his face felt hot and flustered, he smiled more, he observed everything more closely and listened more carefully. His posture was more erect and he had a powerful surge of energy.

Turned off at First Sight

My client Jennifer, a thirty-eight-year-old human resources director, found herself at a dinner party seated next to a man who made her feel antsy and uncomfortable. Every time he leaned toward her, Jennifer automatically drew back. The man talked nonstop, telling long stories about himself. He made cutting remarks about the food and spoke sharply to the waiters.

The two hours Jennifer was trapped in her seat beside this toxic terror were sheer torture. Her energy was drained and her jaw ached from clenching it so hard. Her neck and her upper back were sore with muscle tension. Her stomach was tied in knots and her head throbbed. By the end of the evening, she felt like calling 911 so she could get an ambulance to take her home.

What was it about these two scenarios that made Steven and Jennifer react as they did? What was the objective data that made Steven uncontrollably drawn to the woman at the party and what was it about Jessica's dinner companion that literally turned her stomach? What emotions were triggered? What signals were being received by the brain to cause such strong reactions? What was happening to their bodies physically?

When we feel such strong vibes, we rarely ask ourselves why, or even think about the reasons. In fact, most of us aren't aware how or why we feel as we do about others. We have no clue that behind every person is an objective set of explanations—a full story that can be read through a person's voice, speech, face, and body movements.

Translating the Vibe

If that little voice inside tells you something doesn't look right, sound right, or feel right, that little voice is probably right. Listen to it! Your body knows it. You can feel it in your stomach. Your body has had a visceral reaction, so pay attention—it is the truth.

There are embezzlers, forgers, and Don Juans. There are toxic people out there who will lie to get what they want. They may look fine. They may be well dressed and well spoken, but there will be signs that give them away. We will learn about these signs as we discuss how to determine if a person is lying.

A word of caution: some people are very good liars. The sociopaths of the world often seem to have it all together, but if you listen closely to their speech code, you will note that this is where they begin to fall apart. Thus it is extremely important to be fully aware of your surroundings as well as the people around you, and always to look and listen for all four codes of communication: speech, vocal, body, and facial.

Be aware of what people say as well as how they look and sound when they talk. Don't see and hear what you want to see and hear. Look at and listen to what is actually said. It will ultimately save you plenty of time and trouble.

CHAPTER 3

The Basics of Reading People

Think how wonderful life would be if you could recognize whether someone had a positive or a negative effect upon you, or whether the person really liked or loved you. Wouldn't it be valuable to know if someone was lying or genuinely had your best interests at heart?

While most people believe that you're hearing your inner voice or trusting your instinct or your gut is an inexplicable phenomenon, it is not. It is a concrete, neurobiological experience that comes by paying close attention to the four codes of communication—speech, voice, body and facial language—which I will be explaining in greater detail throughout this book.

The ability to harness the skill of reading others is not an art. It is a science. It is heightened awareness that comes from being in tune with one's senses. Emotions such as fear, anger, and happiness originate in the brain, which controls how those feelings are communicated via speech and facial expression. A person's voice, tone, posture or body stance, and facial expressions are the result of the brain's intricate wiring.

The Four Codes of Communication

There are four primary codes of communication, which are processed in the brain. Two of these, the speech and vocal codes, are processed auditorily, while the other two, facial and body language codes, are processed visually. This chapter provides an overview of these codes; chapters 5–8 will explore them in more depth.

Although different areas of the brain are utilized to process the information received in these codes of communication, the brain arrives at an assessment of how one reacts to these codes emotionally. The result is that all the codes are integrated to form a personality profile of an individual.

Next, the internal aspect of the brain begins to make an assessment whether someone is suited for us based on the emotional assessment of the individual's personality type. These codes provide a clearer picture of one of the fourteen personality profiles we will discuss later, in Chapter 9. When deciphering these codes, I am talking about vocal and speaking behaviors, movements in our body and facial language we can do something about.

To make judgments solely on physical appearance as the early literature on this subject did is extremely dangerous and perpetuates prejudice. That is not what this book is about. This book is designed to help people, not to alienate them. It will help you recognize signs others transmit, which can work for you or against you. You will discover behavior in others that you can or cannot tolerate, depending upon your own personality. It will help you make the right decisions as to who should be in your life.

Listening to the Speaking Code

How you sound provides only some of the clues to inner reality; the words you use and what you actually *say* when you speak are also important. What do people really mean by what they say? Are they sincere? Do they give backhanded compliments (uttering pleasantries that deep down are really cutting remarks)? Do they gossip about you? Do they constantly speak about themselves? What is their grammar and vocabulary like? What are they really saying between the lines?

Hearing the Vocal Code

The way you sound is an important clue to the way you are. You experience this when you answer the telephone. In an instant, you detect a mood coming from the voice on the other end. The vocal code pertains to the tone of voice. Many aspects are familiar, but you may not have paid close attention. They involve the pitch of a person's voice (whether it is high or low), the quality of the voice (whether the person mumbles, trails off, is whiny, harsh, gravely, hoarse, breathy, melodious, rich, resonant, dull, lifeless, enthusiastic, agitated, attacking, sickeningly sweet, or sing-songy), and the volume and rate of speech, primarily dealing with the mechanical aspects of a person's speaking pattern.

Watching the Body Language Code

The body language code is like a personal blueprint, showing how one walks, sits, and stands. Posture of the head is an essential component in analyzing the body language code, as is the use of the arms and legs. For example, how much space does a person use when sitting, or how close does he or she stand next to you?

Looking at the Facial Code

Every face has an expression and we read people from their faces. The facial code reflects how a person holds his or her face when listening and speaking. Eye contact is as crucial, as is how a person controls the mouth. Does he or she keep the mouth open when listening or purse the lips? Does the person furrow the brow, look away, break eye contact? Paying close attention to facial expression can open a new world in reading what a person is really saying. Each of these behaviors speak volumes about someone.

Later, I will explain what can be learned about people from their facial expressions. We will evaluate patterns, such as what it means when a person has a clenched or tense jaw, an aloof or deadpan expression, or an overly animated expression. We will learn the significance of blushing or blanching, staring, and facial twitches, and will see what it means when the eyes are open wide when someone is speaking, when the eyes wander, the lips are licked or chewed, and the nose is wrinkled. And we will learn what it means to have a confident facial expression.

Read Them, Heed Them

It is essential that you accurately identify the underlying emotional tone in each situation. You will be able to employ the codes of facial activities and body language so you quickly identify the negative tones in any situation. That way, you don't get hurt—*emotionally slapped.*

While it is good to be open-minded, I strongly urge you to be very wary of those who set off your alarm systems. Whether you like it or not, there are toxic people who can harm you. These people have personality traits that can be detrimental to your well-being and hazardous to your health. This is natural—we don't have to like and feel good about everyone, just as everyone doesn't have to like and feel good about us.

The first thing you need to ask yourself after you have read someone is *How do they make me feel—good or bad?* Answering this simple question can save you a lot of grief. Most people never dream of asking such a question, let alone doing anything about it. If a person consistently makes you feel bad, you have to ask why you'd want to be around them. If you are deciding whether to do business with someone, for instance, and you ask yourself this simple question, you will be doing yourself a huge favor in the long run.

Using Your Brain

Emotional and Vocal Leakage

A recent discovery has revealed that the cranial nerves, located within the brain, control *both* facial expression and vocal expression. That means the same cranial stimuli that trigger our facial expressions also control our vocal expressions. This is manifested in what I call *vocal leakage.* Even if you are trying to hide your feelings, your true emotions will "leak" in both your facial expressions and your voice.

You and Your Neuroconnections

Consider a person who suffers a stroke that affects the area on the left side of the brain that controls speech. When this area is damaged, the brain has to work extra hard and call upon crossover areas of the brain to compensate. As a result, when the person who has had a stroke speaks, words come out labored, halting, and repetitive. The person must tap into the right neural connections to hear the words, translate the meaning, think what to say, and have the speech areas stimulate various neuropathways to control facial muscles. To a lesser extent a liar is performing the same neural dance, although it takes much more skill to recognize it.

Imagine being so in tune with your senses that you can easily detect such tiny shifts—whether they occur as a flash of movement in a person's expression or a change in vocal pattern—to know exactly what a person means. You will learn how to quickly read messages that others are trying to convey, even though they may not want you to know. Even the chronically clueless can learn to read the messages by understanding the four codes of communication.

There Is Only One Brain, Not Two

Many misconceptions have been perpetuated by writers of self-help books, especially those on gender differences. I refer particularly to discussions about the "right" brain and "left" brain. The left side has been referred to as the "female" brain and the right side as the "male" brain. This information is both erroneous and misguided. In fact, the brain functions as a complex integrated unit, containing two hemispheres, a left and a right, which are *not* separate entities.

The brain is covered by an outer layer called the cortex. There are four lobes, or areas, of the brain, each of which has different responsibilities: the frontal lobe is responsible for reasoning; the partial lobe is responsible for sensory inputs; the occipital lobe is responsible for sight; and the temporal lobe is responsible for speech memory, language, and hearing. Research shows, however, that many functions cross over.

Voice and speech patterns emanate primarily from the left side of the brain, which is responsible for speech and language, from regions in the brain called Broca's area and Wernicke's area. An area located deep within the brain called the limbic system (housing the sympathetic and parasympathetic nervous systems) enables us to have specific emotional responses when we listen to certain voices, hear certain tones, or see people we know or don't know. Some of these emotional responses may be positive, others negative. The limbic system allows us to feel emotions such as anger, love, excitement, disgust, rage, and sadness. Certain sounds, tones, and words may bring out the worst in a person while other people's tones and words may elicit positive emotional feelings.

Use More of Your Brain

Researchers who study the concept of meditation have determined that there is an enormous potential of untapped resource in the brain, which is stimulated through the focus and concentration of meditative techniques. When we uncover the mysteries of the working brain and learn more about its anatomy and function, we begin to understand that if we develop certain areas, we will become more productive in our daily lives.

By learning to access and stimulate the emotional centers of our brain, we can begin to live a richer and more advantaged life. We will detect certain danger signals a lot faster, determine who is the right mate for us, or sense who is trying to cheat us.

We need to become more conscious of how our brain operates and integrate both areas of our brain: the upper portion of our brain, the cortex, where we objectively see and hear information, and the lower part of our brain, the limbic system, where we feel the emotions we see and hear. We do this by training ourselves to be aware of what we are feeling. This will be invaluable to us in the long run.

Mrs. Jones hears her husband's attacking tone in the upper portion of her brain. She processes the information in her left hemisphere, where she realizes, intellectually, that he is wrongly interpreting what she has said. With that part of her brain, she visually sees the makeup on his collar and the credit card calls to another woman.

Now, with the deeper area of her brain, she is able to feel the emotions of everything she objectively saw and heard. She feels the anger of his betrayal, the jealousy over another woman, and the sadness that their marriage is over. As she integrates the two parts of her brain simultaneously, she quickly gets in touch with her emotions.

Don't Get Emotionally Slapped!

Reading a person is a highly emotional experience. It is not enough to determine the codes of behavior and analyze the person's personality type. You have to determine whether you like or dislike that personality type and what it does to you emotionally. You must decide whether that person remains in your life or not.

All too often, we refuse to pay attention to our feelings. Many people don't know how to do this. It can be overwhelming, especially when you haven't been conditioned. Some people have been raised in families where it was taboo to express their emotions, while in other families it was considered bad if you didn't express them.

Even though we have the neurological capacity to react when we see or hear something we like or dislike, we often fail to do so. We may even react days or weeks later to something negative.

Why don't most of us react *immediately* when something isn't right? Why do we wait until it's too late? Why do we make the same mistake in picking the wrong person? We were emotionally slapped—stunned into inaction by the situation.

If someone walked up to you and unexpectedly slapped you in the face, you would undoubtedly be shocked, perhaps so stunned you couldn't move. That is exactly what happens when people are emotionally slapped, stung by someone who says things that are rude and degrading. Sometimes your responses to what they say and do aren't as quick as you'd like. You wish you could have that snappy comeback, but instead you react three days later. That's when you finally realize what the person really meant.

We are shocked when we are emotionally slapped, because most of us can't believe it is happening to us. That is why so many of us become emotionally numb and don't react at all.

With a Friend Like That, Who Needs Enemies?

Paul has known Sandra for more than fifteen years. They have done business together and treated each other with respect. They always asked about the other's family and made nice small talk. They even exchanged Christmas gifts and had each other's families over for dinner.

Paul went out of his way to do Sandra numerous favors. In fact, he was the one who told her about a job opening at a new company. She got the job and wound up tripling her salary.

Paul couldn't count the number of times he dropped what he was doing to help Sandra, even if it didn't benefit Paul in any way. He didn't mind. He was just a friend—a good person. And that is what friends and good people do. Besides, he thought, if he ever were in a bind, Sandra would certainly do the same for him.

In time, Paul needed that favor. He wanted her to make a call to someone he knew, a business contact. Paul would call the person and tell the person to expect a call from Sandra. She, in turn, would say some nice things about Paul. That's all.

When Paul asked for the favor, he watched Sandra's body stiffen, her mouth droop, her forehead furl, her eyebrows knit together. Then she cleared her throat. He realized she would never make that call.

He had improved the quality of Sandra's life by alerting her to a better job and doing many small favors, but she was too selfish to reciprocate. That experience was an emotional slap.

Green-Eyed Jealous Monster Strikes Again

Maureen and Julie had been friends since childhood. Maureen told Julie she was getting married to a lovely man. She couldn't believe her eyes or ears when Julie replied in a matter-of-fact monotone, "That's nice." Then she swallowed hard and gave Maureen a tense smile, with no teeth showing and a deadpan facial expression.

Translation: "I am so jealous of you, I can't stand it. I am just thinking of myself and really don't care about your happiness!" Maureen definitely got the message. She felt numb. She didn't know what to do or say. She was emotionally slapped.

Like the people in these scenarios, we become so numb from the shock of the experience, we ignore the event itself. Then, when we finally come to and realize what has happened, we feel the emotional pain, and it can be excruciating. Sometimes we cannot bear to experience the pain, so we choose to ignore it. We pretend it never happened. If we keep doing this, we can literally make ourselves sick.

Feel the Signs

Most of us aren't really that surprised when we suspect something negative is going to happen and it finally materializes. If we are aware of reading a person's facial or body language, or their speech or voice patterns, we know what's about to happen. We know we are going to get fired before it happens. We heard it in our boss's tone, or even the secretary's.

Chip knew his boss was going to fire him by the way Lola, his boss's secretary, greeted him on the phone. She used to be so happy when she heard Chip's voice. Now she had a downward-inflected, curt tone. As he listened, he knew what was going to happen.

He believed it was only a matter of time until he would hear the bad news. He remembered there had been a lot more physical distance between him and his boss. Normally, there was a lot of touching, backslapping, and kidding around.

The boss hardly looked in Chip's direction anymore. His expression was tense, especially around the eyes and the sides of the mouth. He had little to say to Chip, where there used to be a flood of words spewing from his lips. So when Chip was told his services would no longer be needed, even though he felt disappointed and hurt, he wasn't surprised.

Chip was prepared because he used his whole brain and perceived the entire situation. He knew what to expect. He used the parts of his brain responsible for seeing and hearing negative messages he got from his boss and the secretary. He used the internal aspects of his brain to let him know what he was feeling.

The sooner you tap into the maximum capacity of your brain, the sooner you will be able to deal with the truth in reading others.

CHAPTER 4

Increasing Your People Reading Skills

People Reading Survey

See if you know what it takes to be proficient at reading others. Below you will find a series of questions, each with two answers. Pick the answer with which you identify.

1. How do you handle the past?
   a. You learn quickly from past experiences.
   b. You ignore the past and look at each situation individually and separately.
2. How well do you listen to people?
   a. You listen carefully to what people say and weigh every word.
   b. You often forget what people tell you, but remember the general idea of what they said.
3. How attentive are you?

    a. You are highly detail-oriented and pay attention to every-
       thing around you.

    b) You don't pay attention to little things, but seem to grasp
       the big picture.

4. How do you express your emotions?

    a. You express your emotions freely.

    b. Although you feel your emotions, you do not always ex-
       press them, and often keep them inside.

5. How do you approach people?

    a. You seem to be accepting and loving to everyone around
       you.

    b. You are the type who is cautious around people and doubt
       a lot of them.

6. How do you cope?

    a. You know that, whatever happens, you are a survivor.

    b. You know if certain negative things happen you often
       question how you will survive.

7. What makes you happy?

    a. You usually get a lot of joy experiencing the small plea-
       sures of life.

    b. You are only happy when major or exciting things happen
       to you.

8. How aware of others are you?

    a. You always seem to know the kind of person you are deal-
       ing with.

    b. You don't usually know the type of person you are dealing
       with and are often disappointed by others.

9. How aware are you in business?

    a. You have made more good business decisions than bad ones.

    b. You have made more bad business decisions than good
       ones.

10. How do you make decisions?

    a. You usually make your decisions on your own and listen
       to yourself.

b. You usually make your decisions after listening to others, then taking their advice.

11. What kind of relationships do you have?
    a. You have a lot of close, personal relationships with friends.
    b. You have many acquaintances, but don't let yourself get too close to many people.

What Your Answers Mean

If most of the statements you chose tended to be in the "a" category rather than in the "b" category, you are on the road to being a great people reader. If you chose 11 a's, then you are an outstanding and astute individual who is highly intuitive and aware and who will do very well throughout your life.

Those with 9 or 10 a's are still in good standing.

Those who received 6, 7, or 8 a's are average people readers and need some work developing their skills.

Those with a score of 3, 4, or 5 a's need a lot of work when it comes to understanding others. They have often made more mistakes than they care to admit and have no idea about why they keep making the same mistakes.

Those who scored 1 or 2 a's are in big trouble. They are walking around with blinders on and always seem to be victimized by others. As a result, their self-esteem has suffered greatly.

The Ten Characteristics of Great People Readers

People who read others well trust their instincts and have a lot in common. Here are some traits they possess. Make it your goal to learn and use these traits.

1. They learn from past experiences and don't seem to make the same mistake twice. They vividly remember how they

felt during negative encounters. The negative emotional reaction is so powerful that they make sure it never happens again.

2. They pay extremely close attention to whatever people say, how they say it, and how they look when they say it. This makes it much easier for them to remember exactly what others say.

3. They are constantly on the lookout for a person's reactions—body movements, specific gestures, and facial language—so they know how the other person feels about them, and how they feel about the other person.

4. They aren't afraid to express the full range of their emotions, from anger to love to fear to boredom, since they are well aware of how they feel in any given situation.

5. They are so conscious of everything that occurs around them, they often avoid being victims of potentially dangerous and life-threatening situations.

6. They know they are winners and are quite secure in that knowledge. They know that not only will they survive, they will thrive because they know to surround themselves with supportive people.

7. They pay close attention to small details and see the big picture and are able to experience even the smallest pleasures of life.

8. They have good memories, which they develop by paying close attention to what is going on around them and knowing before whom they stand.

9. They usually make more good business decisions than bad ones. The risks they tend to take are calculated and thought out, since they are conscious of more detail and options available to them. They aren't affected by peer pressure.

10. They have sincere and solid friendships and closer interpersonal relationships because they are in touch with oth-

ers' reactions. They are better able to express their feelings and emotions, which tends to solidify relationships. Because of their acute awareness, they are less likely to select friends and mates in their lives who could cause them a great deal of grief and aggravation.

Remember, knowledge is power. Now that you have the knowledge of what constitutes a person who trusts his or her instincts and knows how to read people, continue to refer to this book.

In so doing, you will find that you dramatically improve your understanding of what others really mean and who they really are. The more you put your knowledge into action, the easier it will get to separate "contenders" from "pretenders" based on those first ten seconds in which you observe another person. It will seem as though you have X-ray vision.

In this chapter, I will share with you numerous exercises that will help you develop your skills as a people reader, just as I have taught my clients in my private practice throughout the years. These exercises are designed to develop your awareness of others. They are devoted to providing you with a keener insight into your abilities to see what people do and hear what people say. The more you practice these exercises, the more proficient you will become at reading people and knowing what they are really thinking. The more you develop your people reading skills, the more insight you will have into people, and your life will improve dramatically.

How to *Stop, Look,* and *Listen*

We were taught to do these three simple things back in grade school as it applied to traffic. We were taught to *stop* at the sign, *look* for oncoming cars, and *listen* for further cars. Failure to obey these simple rules could put our lives in jeopardy. We could get hit by a car. If we do not take the time to do these three things and just blindly walk across the street, we are taking a huge risk and setting ourselves up for danger.

What if we applied the same principles to dealing with people? If we don't take the time to *stop, look,* and *listen,* we are putting our lives in harm's way. We could be emotionally destroyed by someone.

Most of us could have avoided interpersonal disaster if we had taken the time to *stop* for a moment, *look* at another's facial and body language, and *listen* to what they said and how they said it, as well as listening to how we answered the question "Does that person make me feel good or bad?"

If we learn to *stop, look,* and *listen* before launching into relationships in both our personal and professional lives, we wouldn't have to spend another night tossing and turning, regretting one bad decision or another.

The following exercise is the first step. It may feel awkward the first few times you do it, but eventually it will become perfectly natural and you will be able to do an instant reading of people in almost any situation.

Exercise 1: Musical Chairs

It is essential to break the process down simply and go through it frame by frame in order to make it easy to understand. Do you remember when you were a little child and you played musical chairs? You marched yourself around those little tiny chairs while that familiar music with which you perhaps sang along played in the background.

Suddenly, the music stopped and you were told to freeze. You squealed with joy if your body happened to be situated in front of a chair. Or your heart sank with the beginnings of one of the many disappointments that would appear in your life. You probably cried when you noticed that you weren't positioned in front of a chair. You were now out of the game.

The moment of freezing allowed you to

had a chair behind you so that you could cont

not be disqualified. The same holds true for ln

and freeze mentally for a few seconds when yo

another person so you can see who that person rea.

won't be disqualified from living a happy and peaceful m.

another's grief.

Think of the musical chairs analogy whenever you encounter a person. Freeze! Take the time to see if there is a figurative chair behind you: is there an emotionally solid person standing there, or someone whose foundation can be pulled out from under you? Take the time to absorb who that person really is.

Here are the steps. Mentally say to yourself "Freeze!" Sometimes doing something simple enables you to participate and move on to the next step so you can accomplish the task at hand.

Take a small breath in through your mouth for two seconds. Hold it for two seconds. As you exhale, blow out all the prejudices and preconceptions about the person from your mind so that you can clearly input all of the information that you will be picking up both visually and aurally.

Directly face the person as you continue to breathe in through your nose for two seconds. Hold it for two seconds, then exhale through your mouth as you start the process of absorbing visual information about them.

As the person speaks to you, continue this breathing pattern until you are comfortably out of breath. As you inhale through your nose for three seconds, absorb what the person is doing with his or her posture, stance, body, arms, hands, and face. As you exhale through your mouth, be sure to listen to what the person is saying and to the sound of the voice.

Now, breathe in again through your mouth, and this time consider your feelings about the person. Does this person make you feel good or bad?

Exercise 2: The Observer

Here is a great exercise to use the next time you are at a social function where you don't know many of the people. First, relax your body. Pretend that you are observing characters in a movie. This will help you get out of you own self-consciousness and clear your perceptions of emotions. It will help you clarify your thoughts so that you can maintain a clear slate for getting in touch with the emotions you will be experiencing.

Objectively observe the room. Look at the surroundings: the furniture, the carpet, the walls. Now study the people in the room. Take your time; don't overwhelm yourself. One by one, watch how they move and how they speak to one another. Pay close attention to what is happening to your body in terms of your physical responses. What is happening to your rate of breathing? Is it rhythmic? Is it labored? Is it slowing down? Is it fast? Your physical response as measured by your breathing will give you a clue as to how you are feeling among these people. This is especially the case if you have consciously attempted to relax yourself by taking a breath in through your mouth for two seconds, holding it for two seconds and slowly letting it out for ten seconds—the exercise you should do before studying people.

As you watch people pass in front of you, say the first adjective that comes to mind that best describes the person, such as "happy" or "weird" or "blue." It doesn't matter how strange that association is to anyone else, just as long as it makes sense to you. Then determine if it was a positive or a negative adjective—ask yourself if you experienced a positive or a negative feeling when you observed the person.

In doing this exercise, you are training your brain to fully integrate the perceptual part as well as the emotional part.

Exercise 3: Emotional Awareness

After you have met new people and spent time with them and asked yourself whether they had a positive or negative effect on you, go a little further and determine how they specifically make you feel. Ask yourself if they make you feel: Happy? Sad? Angry? Compassionate? Hateful? Loved? Bored? Disgusted? Alive? Dead? Energized? Drained? Sexy? Awful?

After you have come up with an answer, ask yourself one more question: Why do they make me feel that way? For example, let's say Juan, whom you've just met, makes you feel good. You go down the list and discover that it is because he makes you feel "sexy." Now, it's important to ask yourself why Juan has made you feel sexy. You may discover that it was because of how he kept staring in your eyes when he spoke to you, rarely breaking eye contact and because of all of the flattering and polite things he said to you in such dulcet tones.

On the other hand, you may discover that Carrie had a negative effect on you and made you feel very bad. As you go down the list you realize she has left you feeling emotionally drained because she wouldn't stop talking for a minute and she kept telling you one tale of her tragic woes after another. She spoke so fast and in such a frenetic way that it left you ready for a nap.

Stopping, looking, and listening to your emotions and delving into why a person may have an emotional effect upon you may put you on the path of being so alert that you won't allow a person who shouldn't be in your life in the first place even to get near the door. Taking a few moments to get in touch with your emotional state will save you from a lot of grief.

Exercise 4: Photographic Memory

Recall a vacation or an event that occurred six months to a year ago and that you were able to document in photographs, or better yet a videotape. Do not look at the photographs just yet. Now, on a piece of paper, write down everything you can possibly remember about the trip that you took or the event.

For example, let's say you took a cruise. Try to recall what you were wearing on the different days of the cruise and where you went. Recall as much detail as you can, from the hats you wore to whether or not you wore nail polish and if so, what color.

Describe the people you met in detail. Try to remember their names and what they wore. Did they have any unusual features? Did they do anything strange? Did you do anything strange? What did you eat and drink?

After you have written everything down in detail, get the photos or the videotape. Look for details and see how many match what you wrote. How many times were you correct? How was your long-term memory on this occasion?

Many people complain they have terrible memory. But unless they are suffering from a neurological condition or taking medication that is inhibiting their memory, I don't believe most people have terrible memory. I believe people just do not know how to train their memory to make the best use of it. The more you train yourself to be aware of your surroundings, the more aware you will be of your present and past. Your memory will improve dramatically.

Try this exercise six months after you have experienced a special event or an occasion where you have taken photographs or videotape. Write down everything you can remember of the occasion and see how well you match up, based upon the documented evidence in the photos or the video. You will be amazed at how much your memory improves over time as you continue to do this exercise.

The next time you look at a picture of people you know well and want to know them better, carefully observe their facial and body language. Look for signals, such as how far apart they stand. Look to see if they are leaning into one another. Observe whether they appear stiff and rigid. Do they seem uncomfortable being next to one another? Do their smiles seem tense or phony? Do they seem out of place? Is there a sense of awkwardness? What feeling do you get when you look at the photo? Does it make you happy or sad; does it make you want to laugh? Do the people look as though they are having a good time? If you practice looking at people and their photographs and you answer these questions about them, you will be training yourself to read between the lines.

Another good exercise is to look at magazine photos of celebrities. See how close they stand to others and scrutinize their facial expressions and posture. Whether you are looking at photos of your favorite stars, family members, or even at photos of yourself, you will see more than words can ever say about people and their relationships with others.

Exercise 5: It's Movie Time

Studying great performers on screen can help you with your ability to read others. Great actors allow the viewer to get lost in their performances, so you often forget they are acting. It seems so real. You feel as though you are transported into another dimension where the character really lives in his or her fantasy existence.

When you watch one of these great films, don't stop there. Watch the movie again, and this time look carefully to see if you pick up anything you didn't see the first time. You will be amazed at what you'll discover the second time around.

Exercise 6: Turn Off the Sound

Rent a movie and watch a great actor perform with the sound off. When you are just looking at facial expression and body language, you can learn a great deal about the performer. There are no words to cloud the issue. Watch the same scene again and this time do it with sound. See how much more information you get. It'll make a huge difference.

Often, if you want to discover if a politician is telling the truth, turn off the sound on your television. Watch his or her body language and it will tell you a lot. Does the person often bring the hands up to their eyes or mouth? If so, it may be a subconscious attempt to block his or her expression from revealing the truth.

Studying a person's body language will teach you to focus on the nuances of subtle facial expression and shoulder movements, hand and facial gestures, and even how a person sits or walks. The more you do this exercise, the more you will learn. It will force you to become more aware of the emotional state of others based upon how they comport themselves.

Exercise 7: Listen to the Lyrics

A great way to teach yourself to hear what other people are trying to say is to listen to song lyrics. This trains you to become more accustomed to listening to words, rather than to sounds.

Most of us gloss over the words and tend to focus on melodies, but when you concentrate on the lyrics, you will be forced to understand what message the song is trying to deliver. Sometimes you won't understand all the words. But the more you listen to a song, the more you will discover what it's all about.

This auditory training, which you can do at home, in your car, or during any leisure activity, will help you to be on the alert during conversations with others. It will help you become a much better listener.

Exercise 8: A Fly on the Wall

Have you ever been to a party where you didn't know anyone or you felt very uncomfortable or shy? Here's a way to begin to make yourself feel right at home. Just sit there and listen. You don't have to say a word. Simply open your ears and concentrate on what others are saying.

I don't ordinarily recommend eavesdropping on other people's conversations, but if it's done with educational purposes in mind, I am not opposed. As long as you don't use the information against the other person, go ahead and listen.

Listen carefully and objectively, noting people's tone of voice. Listen to their inflection, how loudly or softly they speak. Do they use aggressive or softly modulated tones? How do they speak to one another? Do they tear people down, use sarcasm, or make cutting remarks? Are they competitive, playing a game of verbal one-upmanship? Do they sound as though they genuinely like and respect one another? Is there affection in their tones or an underlying hostility?

By "auditorily" observing the conversations of others, you will develop listening skills that will allow you to read between the lines when people speak. Their tone of voice and the words they use tell you much about them.

Exercise 9: Restaurant Reading

In addition to being enjoyable, reading people in public gives us much insight into how people relate to one another. The more experience you gain in watching strangers interact—their body, facial, vocal, and verbal cues—the more you can apply these skills to your own life.

Let's say you notice a couple sitting at a table, and the woman is glancing around the room with her back pressed against her chair while the man speaks. Meanwhile, the man attentively leans across the table as he speaks. As the evening progresses, it becomes obvious she is clearly not interested in him or she is playing hard to get. Certainly he is the aggressor and is demonstrating it through his body and facial language.

If you observe enough couples, you will learn that when certain distances are kept, or certain head postures, facial expressions, and even arm and hand movements are exhibited, significant meaning is attached.

The next time you go to a restaurant, try to arrive a little early so you can sit at the bar—one of the best observation points—and watch people. You can also practice your people reading skills if you go to lunch or dinner alone. Often, people who are out of town on business hesitate to go to a wonderful restaurant by themselves in a new place and they order room service instead. You don't have to feel that way again. Now you have something to keep you occupied—an endless supply of people to read. The more you practice, the more you'll develop your people reading skills.

If you feel the slightest bit of anxiety at being alone, do a tension blow-out exercise. Breathe in through your mouth for three seconds, then hold your breath for three seconds. Now, blow out the air as quickly as you can. Repeat this three times and you will feel a lot more relaxed. Why? Because your brain will be receiving more oxygen, so you won't feel as tense.

You can practice reading people wherever you are—at the airport, walking in a park, or just standing in line.

Exercise 10: Eliminate the Mental Noise

Before you engage in reading a person, you must center yourself and get focused. There are many ways to achieve the quiet time you need for this. Whether through meditation or getting in touch with the spiritual you, the bottom line is the same. You must eliminate the "mental noise" so you can focus on the person in front of you. You need to release what is physically swirling around you, such as traffic noise, construction, or babies crying.

In order to do this, apply the in-hold-out technique. First, take a breath in through the nose for three seconds, hold it for three seconds, then slowly release the air through the nose for ten seconds. Do this ten times in a row and you will be amazed how relaxed you become. Noises won't bother you and your problems will seem remote.

This exercise also helps to eliminate any bothersome issues that may have occurred in the past, even moments earlier. Many people carry their past into the present and as a result they aren't able to focus and keep a clear, unprejudiced mindset when dealing with issues at hand, or with people they must read. So they are prone to make more mistakes in their observations and emotional assessments of the people they are reading.

For example, let's say you just had a fight with your girlfriend, then you go into an important business meeting carrying that angry emotion with you. Chances are you will have an angry emotional chip on your shoulder and be more likely to react negatively toward your business colleagues.

Eliminate the mental noise and you'll be happier, healthier, and more successful.

PART TWO

Mastering the Four Codes of Communication

Introduction: The People Reading Checklist

Now that you have done your people reading exercises, you are ready to analyze specifically how a person appears in all four areas of communication: speech code, vocal code, body language code, and facial code. In Chapters 5 through 8, I will explain in detail what your findings mean. Chapter 9 provides a personality profile based upon these findings. For now, check either "Yes" or "No" if you observe any of the following characteristics in the person you are reading.

SPEECH CODE	YES	NO
Lisping	_____	_____
Slang	_____	_____
Sarcasm	_____	_____

Speech Code *(continued)*	Yes	No
"I was only kidding"	_____	_____
Limited vocabulary	_____	_____
Limited grammar	_____	_____
Gossiping	_____	_____
Ethnic terms	_____	_____
Cursing	_____	_____
Cutting oneself down	_____	_____
Always talking about oneself	_____	_____
Letting out revealing information	_____	_____
Lecturing at you	_____	_____
"Like, um, you know"	_____	_____
Beating around the bush	_____	_____
Interrupting	_____	_____
Always using big words	_____	_____
Few words	_____	_____
Few opinions or "I don't know"	_____	_____
Speaking in fragments, not finishing sentences	_____	_____
Flirtatious comments	_____	_____
Spitting or drooling when talking	_____	_____
Affected speech	_____	_____
Overly generous with compliments	_____	_____
Words the belie actions	_____	_____
Words in sync with actions	_____	_____
Giggling and laughing a lot	_____	_____
Odd content	_____	_____

Vocal Code	Yes	No
Vocal shakiness	_____	_____
Harsh, gravely tone	_____	_____
Whiny tone	_____	_____
Breathy or flirtatious tone	_____	_____

VOCAL CODE *(continued)*	YES	NO
Mumbling	____	____
Loud talking	____	____
Dying off at the end of sentences	____	____
Overly inflected tone	____	____
Overly sweet tone	____	____
Dull, lifeless, boring tone	____	____
Too-soft tone	____	____
Too-loud tone	____	____
Too-long pause	____	____
Choppy, staccato, clipped tone	____	____
Hard vocal attacks	____	____
Frenetic, manic tone	____	____
Stuttering and stammering	____	____
Speaking too fast	____	____
Speaking too slow	____	____
Angry, agitated tone	____	____
Pitch rising at end of sentences	____	____
Pitch too low	____	____
Pitch too high	____	____
Enthusiastic tone	____	____
Well-modulated tone	____	____

BODY LANGUAGE	YES	NO

Stance

	YES	NO
Standing with confidence	____	____
Standing too close	____	____
Standing too far away	____	____
Rocking side-to-side	____	____

Arms and Hands

Flailing arms	____	____
Excessive hand movement	____	____

BODY LANGUAGE *(continued)*	YES	NO
Too-tightly gripped handshake	_____	_____
Too-loosely gripped handshake	_____	_____
Picking at objects	_____	_____
Self-mutilation	_____	_____
Hunched posture	_____	_____
Overly straight posture	_____	_____

Movement

Clipped, staccato movements	_____	_____
Ridged posture	_____	_____
Sloppy, clumsy movements	_____	_____
Walking too fast	_____	_____
Walking too slow	_____	_____
Making too much noise when walking	_____	_____
Shuffling	_____	_____

FACIAL LANGUAGE	YES	NO
Eye twitches	_____	_____
Staring	_____	_____
Opening eyes wide when speaking	_____	_____
Eye darting	_____	_____
Eyes looking upward	_____	_____
Eyes looking downward	_____	_____
Eye rolling	_____	_____
Lip licking or chewing	_____	_____
Inappropriate laughing or smiling	_____	_____
Clenched, tense jaw	_____	_____
Aloof, deadpan expression	_____	_____
Overly animated expression	_____	_____
Phony smile	_____	_____
Tight-lipped, pulled-back smile	_____	_____
Blushing or blanching	_____	_____

FACIAL LANGUAGE *(continued)*	YES	NO
Frowning	_____	_____
Furrowing of the brow	_____	_____
Squinting	_____	_____
Nose-wrinkling	_____	_____
Confident facial expression	_____	_____
Head cocked to the side	_____	_____
Head bowed over	_____	_____
Jaw jutting forward	_____	_____
Pulling back head	_____	_____

CHAPTER 5

Understanding the Speech Code

Speech Code Survey

In order to analyze effectively what a person says, you need to examine thirty-one traits, which reveal information about the characteristics of people's personalities.

Answer yes or no to the following questions.

1. Do they make derogatory remarks followed by "I was only kidding," after they observe your negative reaction to what they said?
2. Are they "verbally unconscious" and do they seem to be putting their "foot in their mouth" when they speak?
3. Do they seem to contradict everything you say? Are they looking for an argument?
4. Do they cut you down and belittle you?
5. Do they talk and talk until it seems they won't shut up?
6. Do they always seem to gossip, carrying tales about others?

7. Do they flit from topic to topic making it difficult to keep up with them and understand what they say?
8. Do they constantly speak about themselves and have little regard for you during conversation?
9. Do they ask overly personal questions or interrogate you with a barrage of nonstop questions that are basically none of their business?
10. Do they tell you more than you care to know?
11. Are they indirect and evasive—do they beat around the bush and not get to the point, taking forever to tell you something?
12. Are they tactless or shockingly blunt when they speak?
13. Do they put themselves down a lot and are they self-effacing when they speak?
14. Do they usually say "I don't know" whenever you ask something?
15. Do you constantly catch them in lies or stretching the truth?
16. Do they lisp, or have trouble saying their /sh/, /ch/, /j/, /s/, and /z/ sounds?
17. Do they constantly use ethnic words and phrases, even though you may not be familiar with what they are saying?
18. Do they use slang terms?
19. Do they go off on tangents that seem to have little or nothing to do with the subject at hand?
20. Do they stammer or stutter when they speak?
21. Do they mumble?
22. Do they speak in fragments, making it difficult to follow what they are trying to say?
23. Do they hesitate or measure their words carefully before they say something?
24. Are they usually complaining about something?
25. Are they stingy with their words, replies, and conversation? Is it like pulling teeth to get them to speak?
26. Do they seem to be condescending when they speak? Do they appear to be speaking at you instead of with you?

27. Do they try to instigate by saying inflammatory things?
28. Do they nag or harp on things?
29. Do they interrupt a lot? Do they refuse to let you finish your thoughts or allow you to get a word in?
30. Do they constantly use curse words?
31. Are they not interested in what you have to say?

The Score Card

If you answered yes to any of these questions, you have been exposed to a person with "toxic" speaking habits. The more yes answers you have, the more verbally toxic the person is to you.

Now that you have analyzed the person's speech code, you will learn exactly what the answers mean and how they fit into the puzzle as you begin to understand their specific personality profile.

Verbal Leakage

For more than 20 years, I have studied the meaning and subtleties of human voice and speech. Based on my two primary areas of expertise (counseling psychology and communication disorders), I have devised a new, scientifically based concept called verbal leakage.

This is a means by which you can quickly and accurately assess the people in your life without having to rely on instinct and intuition. As researcher Paul Ekman of the University of California, San Francisco, has examined facial "leakage" to visually examine a person's true emotional state, I have utilized vocal and speech leakage to examine auditorally how a person sounds. This approach allows you to use certain vocal and speech characteristics to read people instantly by gaining insights that leak out from their voice and speaking characteristics.

Throughout this chapter I will examine some familiar speech codes so you can identify what they mean when people use them.

This will help you understand the kind of people who use these speech codes as you form a picture of their personality profile later in the book.

You will learn how people communicate by what they say and what that information says about them. You will learn what it means when a person uses sarcasm, flits from topic to topic, constantly interrupts, or seems unable to shut up.

You will discover the characteristics of people who speak in fragments and fail to finish sentences. With information on this type of verbal leakage, you can determine a person's trustworthiness, self-esteem, playfulness, self-centeredness, emotional maturity, and psychological state.

Listen for Revealing Information

My colleague Dr. Paul Cantalupo used to say that if you let people speak long enough, they will tell you everything you need to know about them—and he meant *everything*.

What he was referring to was the art of being a good listener and finding out who people are by allowing them to reveal significant things about themselves. People who reveal risqué and inappropriate things have no ability to withhold. They cannot keep personal information from others because they have no boundaries. If they tell you in graphic detail about their most intimate movements, they are revealing that they may be troubled people with psychological issues you need to know about.

Everything You Need to Know and More

Once, I was looking for a publicist. One candidate I interviewed rarely asked about me and my background, but chose to talk about her own personal life and how she was so in love with a man she'd just met. She kept asking my advice about what she needed to do and say to get this man to really like her. As the conversation progressed, it turned out she was a married woman seeking to spice up her dull and boring marriage.

I did not want to get involved in her personal dilemma, so I suggested she talk with a counselor. Then I directed the topic back to my public relations needs. After a few sentences, she stopped midstream and said, "You know, I really like this guy so much. I don't know what to do. He's such a giving, nurturing, and loving person. I'm not that nurturing because I didn't come from that kind of family, so he is exactly what I need."

I tried to be polite and said that everyone has to do what they must in life and only they can make those decisions. I tried to re-direct the conversation toward my public relations campaign for the third time. But by then she had leaked who she was—an insecure person who was totally unfocused. I learned she desperately needed a lot of nurturing and that is not what I needed from my public relations person.

People will tell everything and you will gain the information you require only if you listen to what is verbally leaked and read between the lines.

The Accurate Side to the Story

My friend Andrea met Bob, a handsome, wealthy, middle-aged entrepreneur she liked a lot. Bob was going through a difficult divorce and told Andrea about his awful ex-wife, how she was such a money monger and how she was cold and unresponsive. He even told Andrea that while he and his soon-to-be ex-wife made love, she would mention she had to go shopping or pick up the laundry. Andrea repeated this story to me as she sang Bob's virtues.

I encouraged Andrea not to be so hasty to blame the ex-wife as it always takes two to tango. I also thought it was embarrassing to tell a prospective lady in his life about the intimacies of his ten-year marriage. I told Andrea, "Perhaps the ex-wife was more inter-ested in going shopping than making love to this man because she felt he wasn't really making love to her. Maybe he wasn't telling her how beautiful and sexy she was. Maybe he wasn't making her feel like a real woman in the bedroom. Maybe Bob was a selfish, self-centered guy who wasn't addressing his wife's needs and that was her only way of dealing with the situation."

"You're right," said Andrea. "I never looked at it that way." Andrea wanted me to meet Bob and we all went out to dinner. At the end of the evening we both read Bob. He continuously verbally leaked information about his ex-wife, how bad she was, how she was taking him for a ride. His money and how much things cost were other popular subjects.

He verbally leaked a lot about his cheapness and stinginess, which was further demonstrated when the bill came and he went over it with a fine-tooth comb. He called the waiter over and said he wouldn't pay for the "cold" cup of coffee at the end of the meal. He then left the waiter a meager tip.

There was a coldness and a meanness about him that was reflected in his facial expression and tone of voice. He sounded whiny and very difficult to listen to. He was clearly a taker who could only function when talking about himself and his money.

He told us everything we needed to know. So it was no wonder his wife was looking for some satisfaction in the department store, because there was no way she was getting any satisfaction in the bedroom.

Verbal Leaks and Speech Codes

Listen for a verbal pattern when people speak. Do they constantly speak ill of others, or do they seem involved in deals where others always get the best of them? Listen to how often they speak of outfoxing another in a business deal. When they speak of others, are they vengeful? Are they always the victim? Do they always get messed over by someone? Are they always in some type of conflict with another person?

The content of what people say is extremely important in terms of who they are as people. Do they speak of things they should not be telling you, but rather a therapist? People you've just met who tell you the most intimate issues in their lives have no boundaries. Instead, they have poor judgment. It's one thing if you are close friends with someone. But discussing an infidelity or an ex-wife's bedroom habits speak volumes about a person, especially if you have only recently met the person.

Following are explanations of the common speech codes.

1. The Great Communicator

People who really have their act together know exactly what to say to others. They are verbally generous with kind words and phases and terms of endearment and politeness. They are sincere and their responses are genuine and heartfelt.

They are honest and they don't have anything to prove. They think before they speak, so they don't wind up putting their feet in their mouths. They are always conscious of what is said and to whom they are speaking. They mean what they say. They are succinct, get to the point, and are easily understood. There is no hidden agenda. What one hears is what one gets.

They are more concerned with the person with whom they are speaking than themselves. This makes them good listeners. They are more concerned about being interested in others than they are worried about being interesting.

Great communicators don't have a need to take center stage. They are self-assured and secure in what they have to say and have nothing to prove to anyone.

They tend to use winning words and phrases such as "perhaps we can," or "it may be in your best interest." There is a sense of cooperation and harmony when they speak as they look toward understanding and compassion. They are sensitive and emotionally secure.

2. The "I Was Only Kidding" Syndrome

People can tell you so much about themselves and how they really feel toward you by what they say to you. If people say sarcastic or rude things, followed by "I was only kidding," they are leaking volumes.

Although these "kidders" may say they are just having a little fun and that you need to lighten up, they are actually revealing hostility or jealousy. People who tease in this fashion may also be trying to undermine behavior that makes them feel uncomfortable, such as dieting or growing older. They are the type of people who don't confront things head on and may express their negative feelings toward you under the guise of cutting humor. In reality, it signals the emergence of suppressed anger toward you, toward themselves, or toward life in general.

"Here, have another donut, you wear it well," said Bob to his girlfriend, followed by "I was only kidding." But Bob was not kidding. He was really angry that his girlfriend, Betsy, was gaining weight. This twenty-pounds-overweight person wasn't the woman he fell for. In his mind, he resented her overeating and wanted the lighter version of Betsy back. He couldn't come right out and say, "I am angry at you for gaining all that weight, because I am not as turned on to you physically as I was when you were thinner."

They Really Don't Like You

Connie was a beautiful woman who looked great for her age. She was celebrating her forty-fifth birthday and had more than fifty people to help her celebrate. Two "friends," Kathleen and Jane, kept taunting her about her age. They kept making seemingly innocent jokes about her "being over the hill." They kept poking fun, telling her she was an old maid now and a has-been.

At first, Connie ignored their comments. She chuckled and reacted in a lighthearted manner by laughingly telling the two to lay off. Throughout the evening, however, they kept chiding Connie. Finally, Connie became embarrassed and insulted by the manner in which her two "friends" kept acting and explicitly told them so.

"Oh, Connie, just lighten up. What's wrong with you? Can't you take a joke? Where's your sense of humor? We're only kidding!" said the "friends."

No, Connie did not see or hear these two harpies kidding. What she heard, verbally leaked by them, were words full of hostility, anger, and jealousy. What she heard were words of meanness. She heard words that were meant to embarrass her in front of others. Instead of hearing words such as, "It's your forty-fifth birthday. Congratulations. You look great, you have a great life ahead of you, you are a wonderful friend. I love you," she heard hostile digs.

Connie tapped into her emotional response to the kidding and determined the truth. These people were jealous of her. They felt hostile toward her and their words revealed their true feelings. They used their "kidding" to mask their true intentions, which were designed to make her feel bad about growing older.

Sarcastic words and statements hurt, no matter who you are. People who make these comments, especially followed by, "I was only kidding," either don't like you or are jealous of you.

They feel insecure about themselves and there is a sense of competitiveness about them. No matter what they say, just remember they were *not* kidding. They meant every word.

3. The Verbally Unconscious

It's not that these people aren't bright; they may just be unaware, or ignorant of certain things. This causes them to lose points in social and business situations. They may be in a time warp and haven't kept up with what is current, or they may speak in slang or curse words because they have a limited verbal repertoire.

I recently saw a gentleman who was in his seventies. He had suffered a slight stroke and needed help regaining his self-confidence and communication skills.

He told me how he had hired a "colored boy." His use of the term told me a lot about him. It said even though he had been a successful businessman, his time had passed. Nobody with any social conscience in this day and age would use such a pejorative term. His limited vocabulary reflected his limited awareness of how the world had changed. It made a lot of sense why he and his son, who now owned the business, were in so much conflict over how the company should be run. This man was decades behind the times.

People who use words that are politically incorrect are revealing volumes about themselves. I remember working with a doctor who kept referring to the nurses in his office as "girls." It showed that he disrespected his staff, which evidently accounted for his high turnover rate. I later learned that this doctor had little regard for women in general.

4. The Contradictor Syndrome

People who contradict everything are "power trippers" who are so threatened they have to show off by saying the opposite and giving more information to enhance their position. By embarrassing others, these people are verbally leaking that they don't respect you. They are very competitive with you and either don't like you or are threatened by you.

This type of behavior is common among siblings close in age, who tend to contradict in order to show up the other one. It also happens frequently among couples who compete with one another.

I remember being invited to join a couple for dinner. It was a very uncomfortable experience because the wife constantly contradicted what her husband was saying. She had to show she had the upper hand by contradicting everything he said.

When he was talking about their trip to Europe, for example, he mentioned he had purchased Louis XIV chairs. "They were *not* Louis XIV chairs!" cried the wife. "They were cheap copies. They were old, ratty chairs I had to spend a fortune to reupholster. Now they look halfway decent!"

Next the husband shared how he loved visiting Florence. "Florence!" the wife exclaimed, "You hated Florence! You couldn't wait to leave! All you kept saying is how sick you were of seeing all of that fancy paper they make over there in those little shops and how expensive everything was, You didn't even go to the museum where Michaelangelo's David was, for God's sake!"

The red-faced, husband retorted, "Well that was the day I got food poisoning and had to stay in bed."

"You didn't have food poisoning," said the wife. "It was because you ate like a pig the night before. You should have seen what this man ate—bowls and bowls of pasta!"

This poor man could not win. Throughout the evening, no matter what he said, his wife had to show him up by saying the opposite. The man was clearly embarrassed, as was everyone sitting at the table. The know-it-all to whom he was married may have gotten her jollies by feeling powerful and superior by contradicting everything he said. But it also screamed that she was insecure, mean-spirited, and disrespectful.

Finally, I could no longer take this scenario, so I politely excused myself. It was clear the woman resented her husband. It came as no surprise when I discovered a year later that the couple had divorced. There was no way a relationship that fostered so much competition and disrespect could ever work.

The husband's next companion was a kind woman who appreciated what he had to say and would never think of contradicting him, especially in front of others.

5. The Cut-You-Downer Syndrome

The cut-you-downer is similar to the contradictor in that they don't respect you or are extremely jealous and threatened by you. These insecure people have to tear others down in order to build themselves up. They need control and power to make themselves feel good.

Let's say you received a raise. Instead of hearing "Congratulations!" or "I'm happy for you," you will hear something like, "Well, I know how good that company is at giving automatic raises as employee incentives."

Perhaps you lost weight after being on a strict diet. You won't hear, "I'm sure it took a lot of discipline and will-power to do what you did." Instead, it will be, "Oh, you lost too much weight! You look so gaunt! Are you ill?" Nothing you tell them is ever good enough. They will always find a verbal black cloud in every sunny sky.

These people don't feel good about themselves, so they try to make you feel worse by cutting you down. They especially like cutting you down in front of others, as it makes them feel more powerful.

People who cut others down usually speak in absolutes such as "never" and "always." They tend to see life as being one way or the other—black or white, yes or no. There are no grays in their palette of options and definitely no maybes. There is an arrogance in the way the person speaks that says it is "their way or the highway."

It is difficult to engage in a dialogue with these individuals because they are usually monologists. They will tell you and talk at you, instead of talking with you. They aren't particularly interested in what you have to say. They don't accept anyone else's opinions and tend to be know-it-alls. They are horrible listeners because they are too busy talking to pay attention to what you have to say. No matter what you say, they have to one-up you or cut you down.

6. The Chatterbox Syndrome

"Shut up! Please shut up already!" was all that went through Jeff's mind as he took Lori to meet his parents for the first time. He wanted them to like her, but for the life of her, she wouldn't shut up. She just couldn't seem to control herself.

People who simply won't shut up are social misfits. Although their loquaciousness may be charming at first, it definitely gets old after the first hour or so. Hearing these nonstop motor mouths ramble on and on about mundane issues such as how they did something like cleaning a sink is enough to drive any sane person up the wall. They generally pay no attention to whether the other person has the time to talk to them.

These people are usually self-consumed and totally unaware of their effect on others. Their modus operandi is often to ask questions, then answer them before the other person has a chance. They simply cannot be subjected to silence because it makes them feel panicky and uneasy. It is as though they have a motor inside that fails to turn off.

They talk in order to comfort or to calm themselves down. This distracts them from negative issues or significant feelings they may have to confront. These people love hearing themselves speak, so often there is a narcissistic element to their personalities. They are more concerned with the pleasure of hearing themselves speak than the discomfort they cause others.

Chatterboxes have a difficult time getting off the phone. They are so unaware that it often takes a blunt, forceful tone to tell them to be quiet—it may even take hanging up.

They are not conscious of how their constant chatter annoys others; they are much too self-absorbed to get the message. They rarely pay attention to any nonverbal or subtle remarks they may get from annoyed listeners. The only thing that will get them to stop talking for a while is if they're told to be quiet in a loud, forceful tone. This usually lasts about a half hour—they just can't seem to control themselves. They must resume talking. They don't seem fazed by harsh remarks made by others since they are so self-absorbed. Even if their feelings are hurt, they'll take a brief break and keep on talking. They are exhausting to be around for any length of time.

These chatterboxes often have a glitch in their childhood psychological development, which may be why they chatter so much into adulthood. The explanation for this behavior lies in a phase of language development that occurs around three and a half to four years of age, when children constantly verbalize to others and to themselves. In this period, they are constantly asking why, even after things are explained time and time again. They do this not only to seek attention, but to hear themselves talk and to express their newly developed language abilities.

As they grow into adults, they may get stuck psychologically and remain in this four-year-old development pattern. Their constant talking may be a psychological defense mechanism to stave off fears of abandonment and of being alone. They need to be around others since they desperately need an audience. But if nobody's around they will talk to themselves and think nothing of it.

Psychotherapy often reveals that these adult chatterboxes were constantly left alone as children. They were either latchkey children who spent hours by themselves or were psychologically alone, ignored by parents and siblings. So they would talk nonstop as a means to entertain themselves in their empty environment. They developed their gift of gab as a means of hanging on to others.

Sometimes hyper-loquaciousness can be associated with drug intake, mental disturbance, or some neurological and genetic syndrome. So one must be aware that some chatterboxes may be suffering from more serious conditions.

7. The Gossiper Syndrome

People who speak ill of others are out of control. They want to feel powerful, so they gossip because they don't feel good about themselves. Gossips are often sneaky and duplicitous, wanting to be your friend mainly to extract information about you and share it with others. They cannot keep a secret and any information you divulge will be shared with everyone in their lives.

Most gossips are jealous and competitive people, who would seek to hurt or destroy you. It's a way of verbally eliminating anyone with whom they compete. As Sigmund Freud once said, "Envy seeks to destroy."

Since these people are envious, they will do whatever they can to tarnish reputations by telling others personal things you would not want them to know. Remember this about gossipers: those who bring information to you will also carry information from you.

You may have thought you said something benign or off the cuff, only to find someone told someone else what you said. In passing, you might have said, "Donna is acting strange," only after the gossiper filled you in on some exciting tidbits. Then Donna lays into you because she heard you were "trashing" her. You try to defend yourself, but Donna is hurt and furious. You weren't the one who said anything negative about her. It was the gossiper. And now the gossiper is telling everyone you said that Donna was weird.

These gossipers observe everything with eagle-eyes and radar ears, so beware what you say to them. They will often distort what you say and carry their distorted version of your comments in their tidal wave of titillating tidbits.

8. The Topic Flitter Syndrome

These people usually have short attention spans and seem to bore easily. They tend to be narcissistic by nature, and are only happy when the topic centers around them or interests them, or if they are controlling the topic. They tend to change the direction of conversation to suit themselves. They are extremely annoying to be around because their conversations are difficult to keep up with. They tend to be selfish and manipulative as they maneuver the talk to address their own needs and interests.

9. The "Me, Myself, and I" Syndrome

These narcissists don't seek a friendly exchange of ideas, but rather have a compulsive need to tell you about themselves and how great they are. They must be the center of attention at all times. They may also be jokesters, telling endless jokes and stories to hold their place in the spotlight.

No matter how boastful these people sound, they are invariably insecure. If they are not the center of attention, they will do anything to gain center stage, regardless of anyone else's needs and feelings. They are extremely selfish and self-serving. Their main concern is to let others know how great they are and they will go to almost any lengths to achieve this. They constantly talk about themselves, their children, their family, ad nauseam. They brag in order to validate themselves in their own minds.

Speaking constantly about oneself is a sign of deep insecurity, a void in the person's development. People who speak about themselves all the time are perceived as thinking they are better than anyone else. In fact, they are merely reflecting their own emptiness and insecurity. They are like children who haven't grown out of the two-year-old "me" phase of development. They still believe that the world revolves around them. If you try to take a toy away from a two-year-old, the child will rebel by screaming, crying, or throwing a tantrum. The same holds true for the "Me, Myself, and I" conversationalists. If you attempt to take the topic away from them, beware! They too, will rebel, becoming angry and verbally vicious toward you for doing so. They don't care that you have an opinion of your own.

A wealthy entrepreneur I know is stuck in this "me" phase. Everything he does and says centers around himself. People refer to him as an egomaniac, which he readily admits to being. What people don't realize is that this man had a difficult relationship with his father, who rarely paid any attention to him. Even when his son did something well (such as excelling in sports or getting good grades), the father continued to ignore him.

As an adult, no matter how much money this man makes, it will never be enough. No matter what woman showers him with love, it is never enough. He is making sure he will never be ignored again, like his father did to him when he was a child. He lets everyone know he is there and he makes sure all conversation focuses on him.

So the next time you hear a lot of "I" in conversation, don't get angry and assume the person is an arrogant, selfish snob. Understand there is a lot of underlying insecurity.

10. The Busybody Syndrome

Like the gossiper, these people have little going on in their lives, so they want to know all about yours. Most of the time, they are very competitive people who are extremely manipulative but the result is that they are rude and not concerned with others. They are privacy invaders, who aren't satisfied with the answers they get. They have to dig deeper into your business.

They catch you off guard by putting you on the defensive. You feel as if you should answer their invasive questions such as "How much did you pay for that?" Or "Is that your natural hair color?" Or "Why did you break up with your boyfriend?"

Since most people don't ask personal questions, you are usually not prepared to answer them. So you automatically tell them what they want to know. Later, you feel like kicking yourself as you say, "Now, why did I tell them that?" It wasn't your fault. They unexpectedly got it out of you by being so rude, blunt, and bold.

Many of these busybodies are likely stuck in the three-year-old developmental pattern—they ask personal questions without regard to what is socially appropriate. A three-year-old can get away with asking, "When are you going to have a baby?" but a thirty-three-year-old can't.

11. The "Tell All" Syndrome

There are people who will tell you *everything* whether you want to know it or not. These people are highly insecure and have no boundaries or limits. In their desire to bond with others by sharing intimacies of their lives, they don't realize they are alienating others. They often become the laughingstock of those to whom they tell all.

These people are also stuck in early psychological development at the two- to five-year-old stage, when children will tell you everything from their eating to their potty habits. For revealing this information, they are usually rewarded by their parents as they hear "Good boy," or "That's a good girl." But as soon as they reach school age, they quickly find out there are some things they cannot discuss, like their bathroom habits. At around the age of five or six children learn from their peers and their teachers that certain things are private. When people reach adulthood and continue to reveal their most private moments, they are looking for that same approval they received as children.

Anita's husband, who was twenty-five years her senior, died unexpectedly. She was beside herself as she was thrust into the dating world after an eighteen-year marriage. It was obvious Anita didn't know what to do and how to behave in the single world as she made faux pas after faux pas. She got involved with men who tried to take advantage of this wealthy young widow.

As her therapist, I was not surprised that Anita told me about her most intimate experiences, everything from how these men performed sexually to the size of their organs to how many orgasms she had. She felt her information was safe because I was a therapist. I would never reveal anything she told me in private.

One afternoon I was having lunch with several people who knew Anita and they began to howl over information Anita had told them. I thought I was the only one who knew these incredibly intimate details of Anita's sex life, but so did Mary and Susan and Lisa and James and Kevin, not to mention the people they told.

Anita's extreme insecurity and lack of boundaries, and her unawareness that you cannot tell all in order to bond with people, made her grist for the gossip mill and the target of ridicule.

12. The Beat-Around-the-Bush Syndrome

When people are not direct and don't get to the point, miscommunication occurs. Women tend to be more guilty of this behavior than men.

When people use convoluted words to make a simple statement, they can cause irreparable damage in relationships. People who beat around the bush tend to be wishy-washy, harbor a great deal of internal fear, and don't want to make waves. They prefer the status quo and rarely take the initiative to make significant change.

Sometimes those who beat around the bush think they are getting their point across, but they fail miserably. A poignant example of this was seen during the Gulf War when the former Ambassador to Iraq, April Glaspie, reported to the Senate Foreign Relations Committee that she took a tough line when she met with Saddam Hussein in Baghdad shortly before his troops invaded Kuwait.

However, the contents of the cable she sent to the State Department to summarize her session with Saddam indicated, according to many senators, that she took "a soft, conciliatory tone" with the dictator. In fact, the late Senator Alan Cranston said publicly that "a stern warning to Saddam Hussein at that time could have prevented the invasion of Kuwait and all the death and destruction it caused."

Perhaps if the former ambassador had been more direct about how the United States would respond to an Iraqi takeover of Kuwait, Saddam Hussein might have gotten a clearer message and might have thought twice before invading.

13. The Too-Blunt Syndrome

While it is a good idea to get to the point, there are those who get to the point too quickly, without using any diplomacy. These people tend to be unaware how their words and comments affect others.

They think nothing of bluntly telling someone that they are wrong or that they don't like them. Either they haven't learned basic social skills or they are stuck in a four- to six-year-old phase of psychological development. Children this age usually say what's on their minds without thinking of the consequences of their words. They may yell out in a public place that someone is too fat, or that they stink.

Although these people are being honest, brutal honesty in adulthood can destroy relationships. In many instances, when adults are brutally honest and fail to consider others' feelings, they may be doing it for effect. They may be bullies who use their bluntness as a form of intimidation to keep others in line. Many football and basketball coaches have used this tactic to intimidate players into doing a better job. But in most cases where bluntness is used, it not only intimidates others but alienates them. Most never forget those brutal words, which remain etched into their minds forever.

14. The Self-Effacing Syndrome

Self-effacing talkers live in fear. Basically, they are afraid of their own shadows. Instead of saying something like "Excuse me" and then asking their question, they may say, "Please, I am so sorry to intrude on you," or "I am terribly disturbed about taking up any of your time but . . ."

This type of speaker suffers from low self-esteem and doesn't want to make waves. People like this behave this way because they don't believe anyone would take the time to speak to them. Often they tend to be people of few words because they don't want to reveal themselves, lest they upset someone. They cannot tolerate being judged and detest being put in the spotlight. They are much more comfortable in the background.

They will never get ahead in life because they won't speak up for what is rightfully theirs. They let others bulldoze them. If others offer support by saying nice things, they will still manage to cut themselves down. Let's say you compliment them about their academic achievements. They might respond with, "Well, it didn't take a lot of brains to do it," or "Anyone could have done it." They always minimize themselves, who they are, and what they have done.

They are frustrating to talk to because they are too busy tearing themselves down to allow you to build them up. They will never accept honest praise from anyone.

When put in a position where the focus is on them, such people can become extremely tense and anxious. Even if they are bright and have a lot to offer, they will often hold back and not say anything, as it may create inner conflict.

What they are good at is rationalizing. They may come up with something like, "Well, what I had to say would sound stupid anyway, so I'm glad I didn't speak up." They will do anything to avoid criticism, yet are very critical of others. This type of communication lends truth to the old saying that when you point a finger at another, there are three fingers pointing back at you. There are definitely three fingers pointing back at the self-effacing communicator. In essence, they are equally as critical of others as they are of themselves.

So the next time you try to give a compliment that is not accepted, to someone who is constantly cutting himself or herself down, this person is probably experiencing mental torture.

A word of caution: these types of people are highly passive-aggressive. Even though they may be extremely angry and justifiably so, they will never let you know it, so be prepared for some subterfuge.

15. The "I Don't Know" Syndrome

There are people out there who are afraid to commit to anything, including their own opinions, for fear of offending someone. Rarely able to take a stance, these people tend to be self-effacing and afraid of making waves. They also tend to be intimidated by people and by life in general.

I was at a dinner party where the man next to me kept saying "I don't know" to every question he was asked. After a while everyone stopped asking him what he thought; in fact, we all stopped talking to him. We found him annoying because he refused to interact with the group. At the end of the evening, he asked if I knew a literary agent or a publisher because he had a great idea for a book.

I was taken aback by his question. There was no way I could recommend this man to anyone unless he revealed who he was. People reveal themselves through sharing opinions and ideas with others.

I told him I didn't feel comfortable doing so and explained why. I said that throughout the evening I tried to get to know him and every time he was asked a question he would reply, "I don't know." I told him it made me feel uncomfortable, as though he had something to hide, or that he was just being a taker without giving any information back.

He replied that he hadn't thought about the things we spoke of and didn't want to upset anyone in case he had a different opinion. He didn't realize that by not providing an opinion he had upset everyone. I then said if he was going to be an author and be able to promote his book, he would have to take a stand on certain issues. Since I didn't see him do this, I didn't feel comfortable sharing my contacts. He appreciated what I had to say and later contacted me to thank me for opening his eyes. He said his "I don't know's" might be the reason he hadn't gotten as far as he would have liked in life. He was right.

By the way, "yeppers" and "nopers" fall into the same category as "I don't knowers." You have to provide feedback if you want to relate to others and "I don't know," "yep," or "nope" just won't do! Such responses reflect a stingy person who is insecure, fearful, and withholds information. This makes the person difficult to trust, let alone be around.

16. The Liar Syndrome

If someone makes a statement such as "Let me be perfectly honest with you," or "I would never lie to you," your initial thought might be, "Why are they telling me they aren't lying? Maybe they are. Otherwise, why would they say something like that?"

Your instincts would be absolutely correct. These verbal re-assurances are used by people who are not forthright. You need to be aware of statements such as these in detecting someone who may not be telling the truth.

People who aren't forthright have both physical and verbal giveaways. They may hesitate at the beginning of sentences so they can process their thoughts and manufacture what they want to say. They also may use "um," "er," and "uh" quite a bit through-out their speaking pattern. They may repeat words and phrases (for example, "I often . . . I often work out.") or repeat partial words (such as "I real—I really liked that."), which they do when they are anxious. Often these repetitions and hesitations occur because people who are not being truthful may not have antici-pated a particular question or response. They may not have worked out the lie they plan to tell ahead of time.

People who speak indirectly, don't get to the point, and give more information than expected also may not be telling the truth. The most cautious lying individual may be caught by what Freud first identified in his 1901 book, *The Psychology of Everyday Life,* as a "slip of the tongue." In essence, people may betray them-selves by forgetting crucial and familiar names or saying some-thing they don't mean to say, like, "I asked him to mate me. I mean meet me." Here, there may be a suppressed thought that is revealed by this slip of the tongue. Perhaps the woman had more on her mind than just an innocent meeting with the man, as she inadvertently revealed.

Another giveaway of the Liar Syndrome is an overindulgence of complimentary terms. If the compliments are too effusive, chances are the intentions may not be honorable. These people sing your praises only to tear you to shreds. While everyone loves a good compliment, nobody likes to be fooled, kissed up to, and patronized. People who do that *always* want something from you.

Confucius knew about these people back in 500 B.C. when he said, "Never trust a person who is fawning." They are opportunists who will drop you like hot potatoes. As soon as something better comes their way or someone else can help their cause, you will be history.

Adrianna, a television producer, would "honey," "sweetie," and "baby" everyone. She would compliment them to death using her sickeningly sweet overinflected tone. But as soon as she got what she wanted, Adrianna would barely speak to the person. Eventually, everybody got wind of her phoniness and she had a difficult time getting hired. People didn't want her around. Her actions belied her phony words.

These insecure people have to make themselves feel important by attempting to manipulate others. So they constantly lie to build themselves up or control others. They want to keep you at arm's length and won't let you find out who they really are, so they manufacture things about their lives or the lives of others to make themselves sound interesting and to maintain control.

Allied to the liar syndrome, is the flirter. These people manipulate others to see whom they can attract and how far they can go. There is nothing wrong with flirting and meaning what you say. A sincere person who showers you with compliments and follows through by asking you out may be quite honorable. But the people who use flirtation as a means of inflating their own egos by manipulating others must be watched. These are the types who have a jolly time teasing you with all sorts of sexual innuendoes and promises with no follow through. They tell you they will call and never do. They are simply attempting to see how many people they can collect who find them sexy, charming, and appealing.

Liars often live in fear of people finding out the truth about them. That is why they are usually overcomplimentary in their words and phrases. They overcompensate verbally but usually have little intent in really knowing you. They use their words as a distancing device.

17. The Lisper Syndrome

People who lisp have a tendency to be immature and psychologically mired in a period of childhood development, much like a person who has a higher-pitched voice.

Dr. Paul Cantalupo observed lisping adults and discovered that those who developed sibilant sounds at the age of six, seven, or eight, were often psychologically stuck in that period of development. He also discovered that people who mispronounce other sounds such as /w/ and /r/ as adults may be psychologically stuck at the age level when those sounds developed. In more than twenty-five years of practice, he observed that young women who lisped as adults often reported having been sexually molested as children, during the time when those sibilant sounds would have developed.

While a person who mispronounces or distorts their /s/, /z/, /j/, and/or /ch/ sounds may sound cute and adorable as a child, it ceases being cute in adulthood. Studies show adults who lisp are perceived as being lazy, sloppy, and not as intelligent.

In discussing people who lisp, we must err on the side of caution, as there is also a high incidence of dental or mouth problems that may cause a person to lisp. So we must always make sure there is no concomitant lisp due to these dental conditions.

18. The Ethnic Flavoring Syndrome

While it is a good thing to be proud of your heritage and ethnic background, it is not good to become so immersed in your culture that you make others who are not of your culture and ethnic background feel uncomfortable.

"So the *shmegegy* over there thought he was a *maiven*. I was just *platzing*. He was *shrying* about all these things, which made me *mishuga*. I finally told him to close his *pisk*. My sister heard what I said to him and was *kvelling* with *nachas* at how I handled the *giferlach* situation."

Translation: "So this nerd (shmegegy) over there thought he knew it all (was a maiven). I was just so angry I was bursting (platzing). He was yelling (shrying) about all these things, which was driving me crazy (mishuga). I finally told him to close his mouth (pisk). My sister heard what I said to him and was bubbling over (kvelling) with happiness (nachas) at how I handled the awful (giferlach) situation."

Unless you understand Yiddish, the paragraph above makes absolutely no sense. Whether you sprinkle Yiddish, Spanish, French, or Chinese words into your speech, it is simply rude to do it with people who are of a different ethnic origin. The key to good communication is to find a common language.

People use these expressions to keep others out and that is wrong. While it may be fine to use certain ethnic terms while speaking to people of the same group as a form of bonding, it is not appropriate to speak that way when talking to anyone else. It is alienating and exclusionary.

19. The Slang Syndrome

People who use slang do so in order to fit in. They are telling you they are cool by using the latest expressions of the day. But the reality with the slang syndrome is that, in an attempt to sound hip and up-to-date, they are *never* totally hip, cool, and up-to-date because slang changes minute by minute, so the person who exhibits the slang syndrome is always behind.

People who use a great deal of slang have an intense desire to belong. They speak as they do to keep others out of their perceived "in group," much like the English Cockney rhyming "slanguage" developed strictly for their peer group. It was formulated as a type of code that very few upper-crust Englishmen could understand. Who would know that "plates of meat" referred to one's feet, "brown bread" meant a person was dead, "Uncle Ned" meant a loaf of bread, and Lillian Gish meant a piece of fish. It

helped the working-class people who spoke it feel special and
unique.

20. The Tangent Syndrome

Beware of those who tell you more than you may wish to know or
who may get off on tangents: they may not be telling the truth.

Gail suspected that her husband of ten years was cheating on
her. She was very upset and came to see me for counseling. Her
husband always came home late and always seemed to have an
excuse. She wanted to know if he was lying about his whereabouts.
The next time he got home late, I told her, she should ask him
where he had been and see if she got a straight answer or if he went
off on a tangent. She did just that. His answer to "Where were
you?" was as follows:

"Oh, I went to the drugstore to pick up a present for you and
then I realized I was out of gas. They didn't have anyone there
who had change so they trusted me to drive over to Fancy's cafe to
get change.

"And you'll never guess who I saw there—my old army
buddy Joe I hadn't seen in twenty years. I told him that he wasn't
looking so good and he told me it was because he and his wife had
just split up. He said he also had a boy who was in trouble with the
law and is now in juvenile hall.

"The poor guy was so upset that I had a few beers with him to
cheer him up. Then I couldn't find my keys, so we spent a good
hour on the floor on our knees, trying to find my keys. We found a
lot of other stuff on that floor, but no keys.

"Finally, I found them in the bathroom and when I went to open
the bathroom door it got stuck. I couldn't get out, so my buddy
wondered what was taking so long. So he comes to the bathroom
door and he practically had to break it down to get me out. Those
bathroom doors are so old. You would think they would fix them. It

took a good half hour to get me out. We were gonna call the fire department to help, but my buddy insisted that he could get the door open, so I let him try."

Gail's husband went off on so many tangents with his bogus story that it was obvious that her suspicions were correct. He was having an affair. All she asked was where he was. He gave her too much information in order to explain away his guilt at being gone for close to three hours. Finally, she asked him point-blank if he was having an affair, which he admitted.

Those with tangent syndrome lose control of what they're saying. They talk endlessly, going off on tangent after tangent to hide the fact that they don't want to state the simple truth.

21. The Stutter/Stammer Syndrome

Everyone has stuttered, or stammered as the British say, when feeling nervous, self-conscious, or intimidated. A stutter often consists of a hesitation, a long pause, or a repetition of words or syllables. Stutterers are often perceived as being nervous, shy, timid, or not telling the truth. Whether this is true depends on the circumstances—when they stutter, the degree of severity of the stuttering and the consistency of the stuttering.

Much has been written about people who stutter or stammer and there is plenty of controversy concerning the topic. Some believe chronic stuttering is due to psychological reasons, while others believe it's due to a child's early conditioning. Still others believe it is due to genetics, while yet another group believes it is a combination of all three. In fact, many speech pathologists cannot even agree on the course of treatment because there are so many points of view on stuttering. But no matter the origin, the problem causes people a great deal of pain and embarrassment.

I am in no way saying that people who have chronic stuttering pathologies are liars. But it is a fact that people who normally exhibit fluent speech patterns may, when engaging in certain lying behaviors, exhibit hesitations, long pauses, and repetition of words or syllables in their speech patterns.

Psychologist Paul Ekman writes about vocal deception clues and refers to people who pause too long or too frequently. They hesitate to speak when it is their turn to talk and stutter too often at the start of a speaking turn, such as "I, I, I mean, I really, I really, really, mean," or they use partial words, such as "I real, I really liked it." Ekman maintains that people who exhibit these hesitations do so because those who lie often haven't worked out their true feelings or decided what they want to say ahead of time. As a result, there is conflict in getting their spoken message across.

Others react negatively when these behaviors happen. They know deep down that something fishy is going on—that these speakers may not be forthright. They don't know exactly what it is, but they sense something just doesn't sound right. They have observed behaviors associated with people who lie. As a result, people may refuse to deal with that person on a business or a personal level.

Unfortunately, that is why stutterers get so much grief from others, even when they are *not* lying. Apparently, their repetitions and hesitations have bad connotations for the human neurobiological mechanism.

This is what happened when Lester Hayes, the former cornerback for the Los Angeles Raiders, intercepted a winning pass that brought his team a Super Bowl victory. The TV cameras descended upon Lester as he verbally hesitated and kept repeating the first syllable of the first word he spoke, over and over again. He couldn't say what he wanted. He could only repeat these sounds. This was the worst nightmare of his life. But it was also embarrassing to the millions of fans who watched him.

Even worse was the sportscaster who unsympathetically kept asking Lester questions as the unblinking camera was focused on him. Everyone felt uncomfortable because the director refused to go to a wide shot and turn off the microphone when Lester was in deep verbal trouble.

The fact that millions witnessed this incident, including significant potential advertisers, cost Lester millions in product endorsements. Nobody believed he could be the spokesperson for any product after that experience.

Ultimately, Lester proved everyone wrong. He came to me to work on his stuttering. We spent hours together, working intensively. Soon he was in control of his stuttering and became a sought-after public speaker.

22. The Mumbler Syndrome

Often, people who mumble have low self-esteem. They may be shy, timid, and fearful, mumbling because they feel that what they have to say is not important. They are unsure about themselves and are hiding something vocally. It may also be a form of verbal passive aggression where they are not saying all that is on their mind.

Esteem issues are key factors in why mumblers mumble. They often experience a high degree of shame and embarrassment about who they are and what they have done with their lives. They prefer to remain inconspicuously in the background so nobody finds them out. The spotlight is something they strenuously avoid.

Because mumblers are constantly asked to speak up and repeat what they said, they are automatically in the spotlight whether they like it or not. They want to be inconspicuous, but when listeners can't understand them, they get annoyed. The mumblers, in turn, are upset because they were brought forward when they wanted to remain back. Thus there is a vicious cycle of tension between listener and mumbler.

In fact it is so annoying that close to 80 percent of the people surveyed by the Gallup Organization found mumbling to be the third most annoying speech habit. We need to use a compassionate, loving tone when we ask people who mumble to speak up, not a harsh tone.

23. The Fragmented Speech Syndrome

The train of thought of some people is extremely difficult to follow. These people are not fully intact mentally or emotionally. They may be suffering from brain dysfunction, chemical imbalance, or drug reaction, or they may have serious psychiatric problems, perhaps even schizophrenia.

When a person speaks constantly in fragments, there is definitely something wrong. Children use fragmented speech while they learn language, which is normal. But this speaking pattern is not normal for adults. Hearing fragmented speech makes us stop and take notice that something is not right. Often this spoken fragmentation will mirror fragmented body movements.

Israeli physiologist Moshe Feldenkrais, in his classic book *The Elusive Obvious,* writes that fragmented body movements are impulsive and incomplete, since one part of the body will be tense while another part of the body will be flaccid at the same time. Similarly, one part of the speech pattern will make sense while another will make no sense at all and follow no linear thought pattern. Instead, speech and thoughts are scattered. Additionally, eye contact is vague, similar to an individual who may be preoccupied.

This off-putting type of speaking pattern is often reflected in schizophrenia, where the emphasis on certain words and phrases and the rate and rhythm of speech are inappropriate.

Beth, a friend of mine, wanted me to meet her boyfriend, Robert, who arrived two hours late. As we spoke, he made no sense. His sentences were disjointed and he didn't have a logical train of thought. I couldn't follow what he said.

When he went to the bathroom, Beth excitedly asked me what I thought of him. I was honest. I said either he's on drugs or there is something terribly wrong with him. He made no sense to me.

Beth became angry and left with Robert when he returned from his bathroom break.

That night I got a call from a crying Beth. "You're right," she said. "He has a drug problem. He told me he was clean and hadn't touched the stuff in years, but I saw him and his friends doing drugs at his apartment, so I left. I just thought he was super-creative and that's why he spoke like that."

When you hear someone speak this way, be alert. It could be due to a number of things, not all of them good. The person may not be operating with all faculties in harmony.

It is also important to note that some people who exhibit illogical thought patterns or fragmented speech may be taking psychotropic drugs for a psychological condition.

24. The Hesitator Syndrome

I mentioned how certain hesitations can be associated with lying behavior. A person may hesitate when busy trying to formulate a lie. The hesitator may also be a timid and insecure individual who doesn't want to make any mistakes, or may be a perfectionist, wanting to get everything right when speaking.

There are also those who hesitate and take their sweet time as a form of arrogance and control. They are making you wait for them to finish. These hesitant talkers are control freaks who believe that what they say is extremely important. So they force you to wait through their long pauses for their gems of wisdom. It is a manipulative device to take three minutes to say what would normally take three seconds.

If you try to interrupt these hesitators, they will often ignore you and continue to speak as though nothing had happened.

When assessing the hesitator, it is essential to be aware of other significant issues. Not all hesitators are lying or attempting to be arrogant and controlling. In this day and age, when so many people are on prescription mood-stabilizing drugs, a new communication issue has emerged. It is not uncommon to find people hesitating midsentence or forgetting what they were going to say more often than usual. If this happens a lot, the person is likely on medication. It can also be a precursor to some serious neuromotor dysfunction, such as dementia.

25. The Chronic Complainer Syndrome

These are the ultimate verbal victims who feel the world owes them a living. They constantly moan and groan about anything and everything. Their conversation centers around how everyone has done them wrong or how bad they feel about something.

Whether it is their health or their relationships with others, they crave attention by seeking help. Yet, when others try to provide that help, they rarely take heed. They find fault in everyone and everything around them. They are unappreciative and self-destructive. They tend to be perpetual worriers who live in the past. Speaking with them for a short period of time zaps your energy. They are downers who can bring everyone to their level of misery.

If you provide them with alternatives, they rarely fail to answer with a "yeah, but." They will always find an excuse about why they can't solve their dilemmas. They seem to enjoy being in victimville. This attitude exasperates and infuriates others, who find their efforts to provide assistance to these people futile.

26. The Few Words Syndrome

Very quiet people often seem scary because it is difficult to know what they are really thinking. They rarely share opinions and ideas, so you are immediately suspicious and tend not to trust them.

If you make a comment such as "Nice car you have," they reply, "Yes, it is." When you ask what kind it is, they respond simply, "Toyota Supra." "How do you like it?" you ask. "Fine," they answer. "What made you decide on it?" you query. "I just liked it." These people offer you nothing other than what you ask. They are poor conversationalists who never initiate a conversation or follow your lead and elaborate on what was asked.

Often, people of few words are dealing with psychological issues. They tend to be extremely shy, self-absorbed, and self-conscious. These people stifle themselves and often repress their true feelings. They tend to deny themselves the ability to discover who they really are and are generally closed to new people, new ideas, and new ventures.

They are aloof and apart, so they don't like to be dependent on others. Instead, they tend to become loners. They live in fear since they can't relate to others. They usually avoid competition. When they are coerced to speak, they often feel they are being punished or tortured. So they speak only when spoken to or when *they* want to speak. They tend to be stubborn individuals who try to control others in their passive-aggressive way by not speaking.

Such people harbor resentment and have a lot of inner rage and hostility. They seem weak and meek and quiet, but they are not that way at all. They tend to be frightening because they keep their feelings so much in check that, inevitably, one day they explode.

In most instances, they clam up because they are afraid of being hurt, due perhaps to trauma in their past. They refuse to participate fully and they distance themselves emotionally.

They are rigid people who can't seem to handle change. They tend to use the same words and phrases over and over, such as "You betcha," "For sure," "I guess," or "I don't know." They often rationalize their one- or two-word responses by deciding that others talk too much, so they preserve words. They attempt to avoid others and justify an attitude of not caring. They often feel hopeless and resigned to their way of life, so they adopt a stance of "Why bother being accepted?" This further restricts communication with others.

27. The Condescending Syndrome

These know-it-all types never listen to or talk with you but instead talk at you. Like a professor or a lecturer, they speak in detached terms or intellectualizations. They tend to be verbal snobs who attempt to make others feel less than they are by talking down to them. They will often overarticulate, use big words, and speak in a slow, deliberate manner, as if conversing with a child.

They often use alienating and threatening words such as "you should" or "you had better," and they irritate others by making them feel disrespected. They will talk down to anyone in order to make themselves feel superior and more valuable. They are not down-to-earth people.

They are impolite and have little regard for others, not caring if someone else is trying to get a word in. They need to keep talking and explaining, pontificating and intellectualizing to get their point across. Should they be interrupted, which they often are, they usually become angry and upset. They feel they are being attacked. On the other hand, they may detach by becoming bored or uninterested.

These people are extremely difficult to communicate with because they are controllers who believe their way is the only way.

28. The Verbal Instigator Syndrome

The verbal instigator, or meddler, tries to make trouble by riling you up. Such people get their kicks out of saying things they know will be upsetting. Their lives are so miserable they try to make others' the same. They communicate by using innuendo to stir up the waters. You may be happily married and know your relationship is rock-solid, but after they get through verbally instigating you, you may have some question about the soundness of the relationship.

"Oh, I'm sure that Tom really adores you and is a completely devoted husband, even though he spent the afternoon with Marcie the other day," they may say, or "I'm not one to pry, but isn't Cleo supposed to be working for you and not Jim? I saw her in his office taking some of his caseload."

These are scary, clandestine, two-faced people who insist on being entertained at your expense. They love to stick their nose into your business and give you advice. They are trouble makers whose clear aim is to tell you something to upset you and make your life miserable.

29. The Nagger Syndrome

These people are primarily controllers. They want to make sure something is done so they will ask you over and over again if it is done. They will constantly harp on you to make sure. They hate to be ignored and will make certain you notice them by annoying you until you do what they say.

They are control freaks who are highly critical of others. When you finally do what they want, it still won't be good enough. They will begin to criticize and point out how you still didn't measure up. Naggers often ask why: "Why do you always do that?" "Why don't you pick up your socks?" "Why must you always say this or that?"

Nagging is the main reason couples end up in therapy and get divorced. It is a mutual power play where nobody wins. If the nagger stopped nagging, there would be a lot more to talk about and less to feel sad and angry about.

30. The Interrupter Syndrome

According to the Gallup Poll, these individuals exhibit the number one most annoying speaking habit. Close to 90 percent of those questioned could not stand it when someone interrupted them while they were speaking. In fact, people who tend to interrupt create a great deal of hostility in others because they do not let them finish their thoughts and ideas.

Interrupters tend to be the ultimate control freaks who bully the conversation by taking over. Their rudeness indicates how self-absorbed and unaware they are. Often, when the person they interrupted gets visibly annoyed with them, they will continue to say what they have to say, disregarding the fact they insulted the other person.

Like the person who flits from topic to topic, interrupters need to be in charge of what is being said. They are selfish, so their need to get their point across is of paramount importance, even more important than relating to and developing rapport with the person with whom they are speaking. They need to have the last word or they will never be satisfied. They need to run the show and to have a lot of attention while doing it.

Deep down, those with the interrupter syndrome are basically fearful people who are so out of control they must try to control everything, including the conversation.

31. The Curser Syndrome

People who use curse words as part of their conversation do it to sound either hip or tough. In many instances it is a defense mechanism used to keep people at bay. If the other person feels comfortable using the same curse words in their vernacular, it can bond people together. Many times people will curse for effect. They want to see how you handle it and what kind of person you are. They may even do it for shock value, as a former client of mine did.

This gentleman had a problem with authority figures and was a known rebel in the show business world. I was well aware of his reputation. When he came to my office, he was prepared to test me. He tried to shock me with his barrage of four-letter words.

What he got was a jolt of his own. Although it is not my style to use curse words, I purposely volleyed some of the four-letter words he used back at him during our seemingly benign conversation.

As soon as he heard these words, a huge smile appeared across his face. "I like you. You are a cool lady," he said. From then on, we bonded. He was basically testing me and was surprised to learn I wasn't uptight and wouldn't judge him, so he felt comfortable in my presence.

Many bullies or control freaks will curse in an attempt to gain power. They do this in order to test, just as the rebellious actor client of mine did. They use it as an attention-getting device to prove their dominance and elicit a reaction. They are much like the five- and six-year-olds who come home from school and tell their parents to f--- themselves after they are told to do something they don't want to do.

The parent is shocked and perhaps angry. "Don't *ever* speak like that again." The child can't believe this little word got such a powerful reaction. Now the child associates these words with power, knowing it will cause a reaction, albeit a negative one. As children continue to develop, they quickly learn that these words have a lot of power and will use them for effect.

I remember a man who had a crush on me. I was also attracted to him until he began cursing. He was actually testing me to see if I would like him if he displayed bad behavior. In fact, I didn't like him as much because the profanity told me this man harbored inner hostility.

While this behavior may have been tolerated in my professional life with my rebellious actor client as a way of establishing rapport, there was no place for it in my personal life. I did not want a man who had to show me how tough and crude he was. I found it embarrassing. It also told me a lot about this man's judgment—it was extremely poor. He didn't really know me and here he was cursing up a storm in my presence. He didn't know if I would be offended and he didn't realize that it was certainly no way to impress a lady.

I also realized that if I had gotten involved with this man and introduced him to professional people, I couldn't be sure his verbal behavior would be appropriate. After all, if he had such poor judgment cursing around me, who's to say he wouldn't use the same language around others? It would be embarrassing to everyone concerned and I didn't want to take that chance.

Now that we've analyzed the speech codes, let's move on to the vocal code.

CHAPTER 6

Understanding the Vocal Code

Vocal Code Survey

In order to analyze a person's vocal code accurately, it is important to realize there are nineteen elements of sound.

1. Does the voice sound too high-pitched?
2. Does the person speak so softly that it is difficult to hear?
3. Does the voice sound shaky or tremulous?
4. Does the person speak too loudly?
5. Does the person sound frenetic or manic when speaking?
6. Does the person speak too fast?
7. Does the person sound angry or agitated?
8. Does the person sound choppy, staccato, or stilted?
9. Does the person "attack" sounds when beginning to speak and during conversation?
10. Does the person trail off at the end of sentences, making it difficult to hear?

11. Does the person whine and sound nasal, even though the jaw moves when the person speaks?
12. Does the person whine and sound nasal and barely move the jaw when speaking?
13. Does the person sound harsh and gravely?
14. Does the person sound dull, boring, and lifeless?
15. Does the person sound sugary sweet with an overly bouncy inflection pattern?
16. Does the pitch of the voice seem to go up when the person finishes a sentence?
17. Does the person speak slowly and deliberately, and overarticulate when pronouncing words?
18. Does the person use a contrived, sexy-sounding voice?
19. Does the person have a deep, rich, enthusiastic voice?

The Mirror of the Soul

Just as a single drop of blood can tell a doctor what is going on physiologically, a single tone of a person's voice can reveal what is happening psychologically.

The ancient Greek physician Galen once said, "It is the voice that mirrors the soul." How right he was. The voice is a significant barometer of how you feel about yourself and the world around you. What you are thinking and feeling generally emerges through the tones you produce as well as the words you choose.

So if we are to adequately assess people's personality characteristics, it is essential to analyze how they sound and what they say in order to arrive at the truth about the individual. Therefore, analyzing the vocal code is an essential ingredient in helping to determine a personality profile.

The sound of someone's voice speaks volumes about state of mind, mental health, and more importantly, how the person feels about you. When Fred droned in a monotone, "I'll call you again soon," coupled with a downwardly inflected tone that dropped off at the word "soon," Roseanne knew she would never hear from him again. That was their first and last date and she was absolutely right.

You probably sense the mood of those you are close to by the way they sound when they answer the telephone. That's because of the inflection pattern in their voice. The nuances others miss are loud and clear to you.

What goes on in your head and in your heart is usually reflected vocally, and when you learn to read vocal nuances, you will immediately have an advantage in interpersonal relationships.

For example, you detect someone is in a bad mood based upon vocal tone. You may want to back off and use more kind and loving tones or you may wish to confront the person and ask if everything is all right. This may allow someone to open up and reveal what is really bothering him or her. The fact that you've been sensitive enough to pick up on emotionally down vocal cues enables you to open up channels of communication.

Before analyzing vocal codes of communication, it is important to examine the evolution of human beings' ability to communicate with one another.

The Voice Doesn't Lie

The voice is the conduit to relaying one's innermost thoughts and feelings. Since the voice is connected to areas in the brain that are involved with emotion, it is difficult to hide vocal changes when certain emotions occur. Because these two are so intimately linked, it is no wonder people automatically sound hopeless, angry, or frustrated when they feel unhappy. Conversely, when they are happy, their voice will sound more alive and have an upward lilt to it.

"Oh, I am so happy for you. I really am," said Randi when she found out Terry had a new fiancé. Randi spoke these words in one sad, monotonous tone. There was no bounce, no hint of excitement for her supposed "good friend." It was obvious she didn't mean it at all. She wasn't happy for Terry.

Studies have shown that personality characteristics and perception of a person are inferred from a vocal and speaking pattern. Those with resonant-sounding voices are perceived as being more intelligent, popular, successful in their careers, and more acceptable for dating and marriage. They are also thought to be friendlier, more sexually exciting, assertive, credible, more likely to be helped, and less likely to be perceived as being "guilty" of having committed a crime.

People who suffer from speaking deficits have had problems with negative perceptions and negative social acceptability. For instance, although women who lisped (problems saying /s/ and /z/ sounds) were seen as being "cute," they were judged as being less intelligent and less competent than nonlisping counterparts. Those with loud voices were perceived as being less likable and more of a show-off than those whose voices were softer.

Numerous studies have explored the effects of voice in relation to cosmetic appearance. One study showed that those who stuttered or stammered were perceived more negatively than those who did not, regardless of their physical appearance. Similarly, it was shown that the perception of nasality was intensified when someone had a facial disfiguration.

My doctoral dissertation at the University of Minnesota, "The Effects of Cosmetic Appearance on Speech on Patients with Orofacial Anomalies," showed that the way a person speaks significantly affects the way a person looks or appears to others.

A person with a facial abnormality but a good speaking voice was perceived as being more physically attractive than someone who has a problem with his or her speaking voice.

The degree of speech distortion didn't matter when it came to the assessment of aesthetics. Conversely, those previously seen as being attractive were subsequently perceived as being unattractive when they were associated with a distortion in their speaking voice.

We've all experienced this in our own lives. How many of us have seen that perfect stranger across the crowded room, only to hear him or her speak and have our fantasies destroyed. That cutesy Betty-Boop voiced woman or that high-pitched, wimpy-sounding man just doesn't do it for us.

Although it may seem superficial, it is reality, like it or not. It is here to stay. Why? Because perceiving the vocal code is a neuro-biological experience. People react viscerally to sound. They either like it or they don't. They either tolerate it or they can't.

This holds true for sounds that emanate from you as well. From ancient Greek philosophers to every major religion to the writings of Freud, it has been observed that one's inner thoughts are usually manifested in one's tone of voice and speaking pattern. These observations have been confirmed today by researchers, including myself, who have explored the relationship between voice and personality traits.

We all know that when people don't fully express their emotions, or try to mask or deny what is creating emotional turmoil within them, headaches, backaches, stomach aches, skin ailments, ulcers, tumors, cancer, and even heart disease can manifest. Usually we can detect underlying tension due to unresolved turmoil by the sound of a person's voice. The voice often sounds emotionless, there is a tension in the vocal muscle, and the pitch of the voice often breaks.

Vocal cues come from the quality, tone, and pattern of the voice. Whether you are conversing face to face or over the telephone, there are definite characteristics that can help you to size people up quickly.

Most of the time we can identify a person's emotional state with a chance accuracy of 60 to 65 percent. This percentage increases when you really listen to the other person. This information is picked up by the emotional portion of your brain located in the inner structures, the limbic system. You store that information in the analytical left side of your brain and even in the right side of your brain so you can call upon it when necessary. As you do this, you will find yourself becoming much more intuitive about a person's vocal pattern and more able to trust your perceptions in dealings with others.

Exceptions in Vocal Code Analysis

Some people exhibit certain patterns in their vocal code that have nothing to do with their personalities or emotional and psychological states. It may be due to something that is learned or genetically inherited.

For example, a person may have developed poor vocal habits because of poor role models and habits. A child may speak loudly and yell harshly at his or her peers or pets after emulating a parent who speaks to him or her in such tones. On the other hand, the child may have a hearing problem that makes him or her speak loudly, or a vocal condition that necessitates straining to make sounds and therefore results in loud speech.

Pathology must never be overlooked when one hears any of the patterns we will discuss in this chapter. I will review some of these conditions so you will have a better understanding, should you encounter them.

Neurological Conditions

A neurological condition can contribute to a person sounding nasal with vocal shakiness (as with Katharine Hepburn in her later years) or to having a nearly inaudible tone that is slow and labored (Muhammad Ali's vocal pattern due to Parkinson's disease).

People with other neurological conditions that make it difficult to coordinate their breathing mechanism with their vocal mechanisms (such as those with cerebral palsy and other neuromotor disorders) may exhibit sudden bursts of loudness when they speak, then taper off at the end of the sentence so you can barely hear what they said. Certain forms of stuttering behavior have neuromotor involvements associated with specific conditions.

Jaw Abnormalities

A jaw abnormality or dental malocclusion may cause problems with tongue placement, proper swallowing, and even lisping.

Hearing Problems

A hearing disorder may contribute to mispronunciation of /r/, /s/, and /z/ sounds. Similarly, a specific accent or dialect can also contribute to these specific misarticulations, as well as a myriad of others.

A hearing problem may also account for someone speaking too softly, since the person may be suffering from sensorineural deafness. On the other hand, if a person speaks too loudly, there may be conductive hearing loss due to obstruction in the middle ear, such as wax or fluid build up.

Dental and Oral Problems

Some people mumble or sound nasal because they are self-conscious of the shape and condition of their teeth, so they don't open their mouths wide enough to speak properly.

People may also have a nasal sound if they are born with a cleft of the hard or soft palate on the roof of their mouth, or have a velopharyngeal insufficiency, whereby the pharynx does not make contact with the soft palate when a person is speaking.

Accents, Dialects, and Culture

There may also be regional reasons why people sound nasal—such as a southern, southwestern, or Minnesota nasal twang.

Speaking too loudly may be a cultural phenomenon, such as when Cantonese people begin speaking English while retaining their familiar intonation. This tends to sound loud and offensive to Westerners, who perceive them as yelling and being angry, when in fact they may be perfectly calm. Speaking softly may also be a cultural phenomenon. Soft-spoken Japanese women are considered pleasant to Japanese, but among Westerners it is considered annoying.

When pitch rises at the end of sentences or the person inflects his or her voice upward, it may be due to a cultural phenomenon, such as a Swedish accent. It could also indicate the use of "uptalk," an affectation commonly used by teens who want to sound "cool" and socially acceptable by their peers.

It is important to note that a person's rate of speaking often has regional considerations. For example, those from New York and New Jersey speak much faster than those from Tennessee and Georgia.

Anatomical, Physiological, and Pathological Concerns

Hoarseness may be due to a growth on the vocal cords—polyps or nodules, or even cancer. There may also be severe irritation and thickening of the cords due to extensive alcohol or cigarette use, which creates the hoarse sound. A bleating sound when people speak may come from protectively tightening their vocal mechanism, usually due to the resulting pain and discomfort of speaking.

A hoarse quality may also indicate the presence of upper respiratory problems. Asthma, bronchitis, emphysema, or chronic obstructive pulmonary dysfunction (COPD) often causes people to have difficulty coordinating their flow of air with their speaking. Usually people who suffer from these problems will take several shallow breaths instead of a larger one to sustain a tone when they speak. This can be annoying to the listener, but cannot be helped, nor can their chronic coughing. Upper respiratory problems may also be the reason why people may trail off at the end of sentences. Upper respiratory distress may once again be the culprit when people talk quickly.

There may be pain in the region of the back of the throat or a postnasal drip that triggers a coughing or a "choking" attack. A person in this condition usually tries to get as much information out as quickly as possible, which they may do by speaking too fast.

A high-pitched voice may also indicate a small vocal apparatus, deformity, or severe damage to the larynx.

People who have a condition known as *spastic dysphonia,* where there is extreme tension and spasticity of the vocal muscles, will usually speak in a labored, choppy pattern.

Drugs

People who take certain narcotics have also been known to manifest a choppy-sounding, spastic type of vocal quality, combined with inappropriate bursts of loudness, indicating a lack of coordination between the respiratory and phonatory mechanisms.

People with drug problems, or those who take certain mood-stabilization drugs, may have a tendency to speak slowly, or pause before moving on, which can reflect short-term memory problems. Certain prescription drugs given to those with bipolar disorder or epilepsy can create short-term memory loss as well as a shaky and tentative-sounding voice quality.

Barbiturate or heroin use can produce a slow and labored pattern of speech, while amphetamines and cocaine can create an extraordinarily rapid rate. Drugs such as cocaine damage the internal mucosa (the lining of their nasal cavities), which allows air to escape, making them sound nasal. Another tell-tale sign is constant sniffling, nose clearing, and nose blowing, which further accounts for the nasal tone.

It is important that each of these factors be considered before any personality trait or behavior is assessed.

As we listen to the voices of others, we must determine whether an individual is particularly stressed, or under a great deal of pressure. That is why it is best to make observations over a period of time and during a variety of circumstances if at all possible.

Analyzing Vocal Cues

The vocal code must be analyzed in four major categories: (1) pitch (high or low); (2) loudness (soft, loud, or fade out at the end); (3) quality (shaky, harsh, gravelly, attacking with sudden bursts of loudness, whiny, nasal, breathy); and (4) style (frenetic-manic, too fast, agitated, choppy and staccato, dull and lifeless, sugary sweet, sexy and flirtatious, too slow, well modulated, pitching up at end of sentences, rich, enthusiastic).

Style

1. The Winning Voice with Deep, Rich, Enthusiastic Tones

A voice that exhibits the right tone says it all. The winning voice quality is perceived as being deeper in both men and women. It provides an expression of sophistication and sexiness and emotional security.

A lively voice maintains a person's interest in you through its enthusiastic and life-filled bounce. It has to have a varied pitch and loudness as well as have a confident tone and timbre. It conveys love, anger, joy, compassion, sadness, fear, doubt. It is a tone that makes people's ears perk up and listen. It is robust and carries the message with ease.

These tones tend to draw people to you like a magnet because they bring out the best in both you and in others. A tone that says, "I have self-confidence" makes others feel confident and communicates trust. People with this type of voice pattern are perceived as being more credible, sexier, more intelligent and trustworthy. They are in control of their lives. Their voice doesn't waiver or falter. Rock-solid people employ this tone and speak with their mind and heart. These people are forthright and have integrity.

It has been said that the late actor Richard Burton could make the phone book sound interesting because of his rich, sonorous voice. It not only made him sound credible but gave him enormous sex appeal.

Women who speak in this rich tone, with an enthusiastic vocal bounce, have been found to have a clear advantage when it comes to attracting others. Their contagious vocal effervescence makes others perceive them as being friendlier, more credible, more capable, and more sexually attractive than women who do not have this type of voice.

When you sound this way, you attract others who find themselves happier and more upbeat when they are in your presence.

Pitch

2. The Too-High-Pitched Voice

Whether male or female, an individual with a high-pitched vocal quality is often associated with immaturity, not being in touch with one's sexuality, being tentative, insecure, weak, and angry. When a person is sexually aroused, the pitch of the voice drops, so a person whose voice remains high may be denying or blocking out his or her sexuality.

In my practice I have helped young women lower the tone of a high-pitched voice. Nearly everyone I worked with who had this problem had a sexual issue, an early childhood or teenage molestation. Often the trauma is so severe that it can stifle emotional development, leaving the person at an emotionally earlier age. My dear friend and colleague, the late psychiatrist and psychoanalyst Dr. Paul Cantalupo, found this trend throughout his twenty-five-year career. He believed emotional growth may have been stifled by the trauma of what the victims experienced, so they became stuck and never evolved vocally.

Juana, a former patient, who was bilingual in English and Spanish, exemplifies what Dr. Drew Pinsky, Dr. Paul Cantalupo, and I am referring to. Juana had a rich and sonorous voice, low in pitch. She exuded confidence. Vocally versatile, she could sound sensuous and sultry and made many voiceovers in English where she called upon that quality. Because she was fluent in Spanish, she tried to add to her income by doing voiceovers for the Spanish marketplace.

But casting agents said her voice was too high. So she came to me for help. No matter how hard we tried and how many techniques we used, we couldn't deepen her pitch when she spoke Spanish. And yet she had this low, flowing voice when speaking English. Something didn't make sense, until I asked her if she'd experienced any trauma in her youth.

Suddenly she broke down and sobbed as she recalled how she was gang-raped when she came to this country from Mexico. She was a young girl at the time, and had never told anyone about the incident due to cultural restraints. This was the first time she had spoken about it.

She associated the trauma with her native tongue. And this was reflected in the high, little-girl pitch. But it was *not* reflected in English, a language with which she did not associate the emotional trauma.

Neither a man nor a woman will be taken seriously with a high-pitched voice. This type of person is perceived as being weaker, not as intelligent or as competent as those with richer-sounding voices. Often when a person is nervous and lacks self-confidence, the vocal muscles tighten, thereby creating a high-pitched tone.

It is a fact that when a person is angry the pitch of the voice rises. In Dr. Paul Ekman's studies on emotion, he found that in about 70 percent of those he studied, pitch went up when they were upset. Therefore, it stands to reason that if a person consistently speaks in a high-pitched voice, he or she may tend to be in a perpetual state of residual anger, internal anger, or even fear.

Through the years, I have worked with thousands of clients on this problem. There are always mechanical exercises, but the key element is to work with them on building confidence levels. This psychological work is essential if people are to turn their lives around.

So, it is possible that, with the right form of voice and psychological therapy, you don't have to be branded with a high-pitched voice.

3. The Very Low-Pitched Voice

Those with thicker vocal cords or a larger vocal apparatus may speak in low-pitched tones. In general, for both men and women, a voice that is lower in pitch is more aesthetic sounding. However, when the pitch is forced at a lower octave, it appears to be contrived. People are perceived as sounding phony or pretentious.

Excessive lowering of the voice often occurs in men who are insecure about themselves. They believe if they speak lower, and oftentimes louder, people will take them more seriously and perceive them as being more powerful. They believe that in lowering their pitch, they will be treated with more respect and that people will listen to them.

As a birthday gift, a client sent her boyfriend to me for a session to evaluate his speech and communication skills. At first he was reluctant to come because he thought he had a great voice and didn't need my services. But since his girlfriend had paid for it, he kept the appointment. He figured his girlfriend was giving him this gift to flatter his ego—that she loved his voice so much, she wanted him to hear from a professional how great he sounded.

When he arrived, he spoke in an extremely low-pitched voice. He told me he thought his voice was a turn-on for women because it was so low and sexy. Little did he know that the reason his girlfriend sent him was because it was a turnoff. She felt he sounded obnoxious and pompous. She was embarrassed to go out in public with him because of the looks people gave them. She didn't know how to tell him his voice was a deal breaker, so she left that unpleasant task to me.

After seeing and hearing a videotape of himself, he finally got the picture. He didn't have to push so hard in order to have a less deep, more natural-sounding voice. I showed him how to find his optimum pitch level and encouraged him to speak in a more natural pitch. That, along with some counseling on improving his self-esteem, changed his pitch. He was happy and so was his girlfriend.

Volume

4. The Too-Soft Voice

The quiet ones get attention by having people ask them to speak up. Deep down, they enjoy this and use it as a power play, to make others strain to hear them. They annoy others who ask them to repeat themselves. They have succeeded in gaining control over a situation in which they previously had no control. Some get wise to this ploy and know what to do to make the perpetrator speak up.

Kathy was sick of Marcie's shy act, which included forcing others to get her to speak up. So, at a meeting, Kathy said to the group leader who fell into Marcie's trap, "Just ignore her, she can't speak. Besides, you'll never hear a word she says anyway, so just talk to me and ask any question you have."

Marcie was livid. She immediately lost it and in the loudest, boldest voice Kathy ever heard, said, "What are you talking about? Of course I can speak!" She never pulled her "shy me" stunt again, at least not in front of Kathy.

These soft talkers aren't what they seem to be. They are the opposite of what they want others to believe. They want to make you think they are shy, innocent, and demure. In reality, you will often experience them flying off the handle and blowing up. It is their power play—all a game.

In my nearly two decades of experience, I have seen this voice quality used as a manipulation technique—a passive-aggressive mechanism that is laden with anger at whatever psychological demons have not yet been worked out and lurk inside of them. It is an attention-getting device. I suggest you be extremely cautious of soft speakers because you, like most, will discover they can be dangerous. They are often the opposite of how they sound.

Researchers who have studied voice and emotion have also discovered that softer speech tends to be associated with sadness. People who speak softly on a consistent basis may, in essence, be harboring some type of internal and deep sadness, just like the person who speaks too loud. Both may be suffering from hidden anger that they harbor deep inside.

The soft speaker often feels powerless, less dominant, and out of control, and often suffers from feeling unworthy of speaking up and being heard. As a result, he or she may use this soft-speaking behavior as a ploy to get others to listen.

5. The Too-Loud Voice

The loud-talker craves attention and will bellow as loudly as he or she can in order to get just that. They are often pompous and arrogant, socially unaware, controlling, bullyish, competitive, angry people with a lot of hostility. Because they are so insecure, they need an audience to hear what they have to say or they cannot function.

Dr. Matthew McKay and Dr. Martha Davis, researchers from the University of California, San Francisco, best describe the loud talker as one who says, "I am in command. Do what I tell you," confirming their bullying attitudes.

Dr. Paul Ekman's research on emotion and the voice also validates my findings that a louder voice is associated with anger. These loud talkers are angry people who exhibit their inner hostility toward others and toward themselves through loud, warlike tones.

Additionally, they often come from large families where they've had to fend for themselves and speak over brothers and sisters just to be heard. This experience often leaves them with a great deal of insecurity since they need to be the center of attention.

Unless a person has a conductive type of hearing loss, where there is fluid or wax buildup or a substance trapped in the middle ear, there is no excuse for someone not to be conscious of how loud he or she is speaking. If there is no hearing loss, you can be sure that loud talking is associated with some type of anger. It could be internal anger, subconsciously harbored by the loud talker, or it could be external anger directed toward anyone. The more insecure they feel, the louder they speak, which can prove to be quite embarrassing.

This happened with a person I knew who usually isn't insecure. But when I took him to dinner at an elegant club, I was shocked at how loud he was talking, especially about personal matters. He was oblivious to others and ignored the annoyed looks he was getting from those at nearby tables. This person felt so insecure and intimidated, he was, in essence, screaming out, "Look at me, I'm important, too. Notice me!"

6. Fading out at the End of Sentences

Like the soft talker, these people often suffer from poor self-esteem. Their vocal pattern displays sloppiness, and a lack of control, preciseness, deliberateness, and follow-through. Lacking self-confidence makes them feel that what they have to say isn't important.

People whose voices die off at the end of sentences generally do not manifest confident breathing skills, inhaling through their mouths and exhaling on their breath while speaking. Since they tend to be easily exasperated, they exhale and then speak, making it difficult to hear them.

Unlike the soft talker, the person whose speech dies off at the end of sentences is not as manipulative and controlling. Instead, these people start out fine but get lost at the end, so there is no follow-through of tone. This may be reflected in their lifestyle—they may be the kind who starts something but doesn't finish it. I have observed many clients who had this type of vocal pattern. They've felt frustrated due to low self-esteem and tended not to complete their tasks.

Maury sought my assistance in preparing a presentation. It was the first time he was going to speak publicly and he didn't know what to do. He had a great speaking voice with a rich, low tone but he tended to trail off at the end of sentences so he could barely be heard. He swallowed his words.

I asked him if he was the sort who started something and never finished. He smiled and said, "That's my life story. You should see my apartment. It's an absolute mess, so much so, a maid wouldn't know where to begin.

"It took me eight years to get through undergraduate school

and there were bets as to whether I'd ever finish. I have a hard time finishing projects at work. In fact, I haven't even finished the speech you're helping me with."

I told him his vocal pattern reflected that behavior and we would try to change things. I said he could not speak until he took a breath in and used his powerfully resonant voice to flow out his entire thought. I told him to stop, take a breath in, and flow out the next thought until he finished everything he wanted to say.

We began practicing and he began to sound fantastic. He wound up giving a brilliant presentation. I also taught him to use the same strategy of taking a breath in and flowing it out to finish every task he undertook. He dramatically changed his vocal code *and* his life by finishing things for the first time.

Quality

7. The Shaky Voice

Those who have vocal shakiness are often upset and nervous. They spend a lot of time worrying what others think of them or what may happen to them. (Note that people on psychotropic medications to maintain mood stability may display a vocal tremor as a result, so be careful not to confuse those who are nervous from those who are medicated.)

Often, those with a tremor in their voices fear life. They are tentative, afraid to jump in and go for it since they are usually overly concerned with the repercussions from any action. They tend to be neurotic and paranoid about who said what to whom, and what will happen. Concerned about living in the future, they avoid living in the present and may be timid about confronting daily issues. They live on shaky ground, as reflected in their shaky vocal quality, and are unable to cope with many of life's stresses.

When these people are put on the spot, they often break out in red blotches or turn red. Their vocal muscles tense up and their voices begin to shake. They are driven by fear and desperately want to fit in. They hunger for approval.

My client Chelsea and I worked extensively on emotional issues. She desperately needed the approval of others, stemming from her father's lack of approval throughout her life. Now for the first time, because she wasn't as hung up on what others thought of her, she was finally able to relax the muscles in her throat, including her vocal muscles. As a result, she didn't sound shaky and nervous. She noticed that people gravitated toward her a lot more and seemed to enjoy her company. People began to smile around her and didn't look so tense.

8. Vocal Attackers

People who "attack" with their tones are often angry, aggressive, and competitive. The attacking tones are manifested in periodic loud bursts of sound peppered throughout a conversation. They are like little shocks of hostility—machine gun blasts of hate or anger spewing forth during communication. These inappropriate, sudden bursts of loudness are jolting to the listener, who may find the tone of rampant vocal attacks incongruous to the topic being discussed.

For example, when discussing something as benign as what someone did over the weekend, a vocal attacker's bursts of verbal gunfire make it sound as though he or she were on a battlefield and had a miserable time when in fact it may have been a pleasant time. But the anger and hostility that plagues this type of person is reflected in the tone.

These people are highly competitive and always seem to be looking for ways to beat their "opponent," even in simple conversation. (An opponent may be anyone with whom they are conversing.) So they must vocally attack first in order to be heard. This gives them the perception of a winning edge.

9. Nasal Whiners Who Move Their Jaws

People with a nasal whine are rarely taken seriously. They are often unfairly judged as being not as intelligent as their nonwhining counterparts. They are also perceived as being unaware of those around them. Their grating voice quality makes them sound obnoxious, as if they are complaining about something—and they usually are. Their tones reflect dissatisfaction. A Gallup Poll found this trait to be one of the seven most annoying speaking habits. Close to 70 percent of the people surveyed found this voice quality to be a turnoff.

Nasal whiners sound as though they want something from you, or something isn't right. They tend to be the brunt of other people's jokes, so they are either extremely defensive and verbally aggressive, or they have learned to laugh at themselves, often playing up their vocal trait and using it to their advantage. Judy Holliday, Edith Bunker *(All in the Family),* and Fran Drescher *(The Nanny)* made careers out of their nasal whines.

Whiners tend to make others laugh. I know I did when Fran Drescher came into my office to get help losing her thick Queens accent. I actually thought someone was playing a joke on me by sending this highly nasal-sounding person. So in the middle of the session, I said to Fran, "All right, you can stop talking like that. Who really sent you here?" She promptly informed me that this was the way she really spoke and that Elaine Rich, her manager, had sent her.

Fran and I worked hard to eliminate her accent, which she did successfully. The down side was that she couldn't get any work in Hollywood with her new, non-nasal voice. So she went back to her old nasal ways and managed to make millions with a hit series.

10. Harsh and Gravelly Voices

One night at a social event I heard a man speak whose voice was harsh and gravelly. It was an uncomfortable experience. My first thought was, I'll bet this man is hard to get along with. Later I found out he was a very difficult man whom nobody cared for. I overheard several of his coworkers share less than favorable stories about the man. Apparently he was a mean, angry bully who always had to have his way. I knew it, I said to myself. He was a harsh graveler: aggressive, controlling, and bossy.

There was a new man in Deanne's life and she wanted me to listen to a message he had left on her phone machine. She had some reservations about this man, who called to ask her out for a date. She didn't know what it was; she just had a funny feeling about him. After listening to his voice, I could see why. He sounded harsh and gravelly. It was grating to the ears. Even though he used such endearing terms as "dear" and "babe," it still sounded unpleasant. She asked for my impressions.

I told Deanne I thought he sounded as though he had a lot of anger and would be a controlling, bossy type of person, a bully. "Yes!" she screamed, "That's it! That's exactly why I feel funny about seeing him. He's a bully. He bullies waiters, his kids, and he even bullies me. He is angry and always complains. If it's not about his partner, it's about his ex-wife or his kids. Frankly, I'm sick of it. And he always has to be right! He's not happy unless he's controlling everything."

A light went on in Deanne's head. She woke up and realized this was not the man for her.

This type of personality has its roots in childhood. An informal study done in several elementary and preschools found that children with harsh, gravelly voices were considered by their teachers to be angry children who were regarded as class bullies. They were also found to be those most disliked by the other children.

11. The Deliberately Sexy, Breathy Voice

When people use that sexy, breathy, seductive purring tone, rest assured they are playing a game. It is especially disappointing when you hear them speak this way with others after they've spoken this way with you. It's insincere, manipulative, and insulting. These people think they can "seduce" another person to do whatever they want. They often have an overinflated ego and feel they are entitled to use others for their own gain. Those with breathy-sounding voices are often not taken seriously. Susan Hayden Elgin, linguistics professor at San Diego State University, says they are often perceived as being untrustworthy.

You immediately hear how phony these sex-toned individuals are when they keep using this voice, even though they find they're making no headway with the person they are trying to seduce. Watch how their voice returns to its normal, nonseductive state when nobody responds.

A dentist I know hired one of these breathy-voiced women to help him as a receptionist. He believed she would add to his image. Instead, she detracted from it. His patients weren't happy with this new receptionist. They simply didn't think she was competent and didn't trust her to put their appointments down on the right day. Nor did they believe she could handle their insurance claims or payments accurately.

Other studies have equated a breathy-sounding voice with being unassertive and lacking confidence. This may also be why the dental receptionist was so poorly perceived.

12. Frenetic, Manic Tones

Alice talks a mile a minute, as though her mouth were a machine gun firing bullets from her throat. She is exhausting and is always in crisis mode. Life is an emotional roller coaster. Her cat got lost, she kept you waiting because she couldn't get a cab, she lost her checkbook, she left her important papers at the bank.

It is always something and she delivers her message by aiming a barrage of verbal bullets directly at your face. At first Alice seems cute and fascinating, intriguing and exciting. You may have even looked forward to the adventures of Alice in Wonder-What-Will-Happen-Next-Land. But this steady diet of "in your face" communication quickly becomes exhausting for those on the receiving end, while revealing a lot about the speaker herself.

This type of person is overbearing, controlling, and must be the center of attention. Heaven help you if you try to turn any of the attention on yourself and discuss any of your own woes. You can be certain she will not be as compassionate as you have been to her. Most likely, one of two things will happen. She will either bring her troubles back into the conversation or she will lash out if you persist talking about yourself. Her point of view is, who cares about you?

Donna experienced this when she tried to share with Alice the trauma of losing her husband to his secretary. Alice was no help— she kept describing to Donna every horrific experience with a man who "did her wrong."

She exhibited no compassion. She hardly let Donna speak. This angered Donna, who let out her emotions. An awful exchange occurred, with Alice accusing Donna of being selfish and only caring about herself when Alice was trying to "help."

These people are usually out-of-control, manipulative, and very selfish. When the content isn't about them, they are not compassionate. There is no give and take in the relationship. Chances are they have deep emotional and mental problems that need to be addressed.

Researchers who have studied voice and emotion have discovered that those who speak at such a rapid rate are usually exhibiting anger. They always seem to be upset at others or in conflict with them. Their rapid-fire, forceful speaking pattern can also be associated with the "pressured speech" phenomenon often seen in people who have bipolar disorder and do not have the disorder under control. Understand that people who speak in this manner may be chemically imbalanced.

That is not to say that all people who speak in a manic and frenetic way suffer from bipolar disorder. The positive side to this type of speaking pattern is that it tends to get others excited. It motivates people to get involved or enroll in their projects. These people are cheerleaders who make just about everything sound interesting. They are exciting to watch because they seem to have boundless energy and enthusiasm for everything they do.

The only problem is that often they don't know what they are talking about, and following their schemes may not be in your best financial or emotional interest. So be careful before you get sucked into something you shouldn't be doing.

13. Talking Too Fast

These people are extremely anxious, nervous, and may be angry. Studies have shown they tend to be insecure and suffer from low self-esteem. That is often why they subconsciously want to hurry up and get it all out. Mainly it is because, deep down, they don't believe others are interested in what they have to say. If they had more self-esteem, they would take the time to allow others to hear the importance of their message. Fast-talkers may also be typical "Type A" personality people, highly driven, ambitious individuals who usually speak aggressively and rapidly.

Fast-talkers are one of the top eight annoying patterns of communication and over 65 percent of the people surveyed in a Gallup Poll were uncomfortable with those who spoke too quickly. They tend to make others feel anxious, according to psychologists Dr. Matthew MacKay and Dr. Martha David of the University of California, San Francisco.

Many fast-talkers come from larger families. This is similar to the loud talker, who needs to be heard above the noise of the other siblings. Fast-talkers believe they must speak rapidly in order to get everything out before they are interrupted.

Studies also show that people who speak faster tend to exhibit more anger. Perhaps there is more stress and anger in competitive environments, such as large families and larger cities, which contribute to this rapid rate of speaking.

14. Agitated Tones

It's not what you say, but how you say it. Ask others in a pleasant tone to do something and they will usually do it. But the person who uses a tone with attitude will generally cause others to rebel, resulting in a verbal fight, or worse—a physical altercation. As the Bible says, "The power of the word rests on the tongue." It also rests on the tone a person uses.

Agitated tones are heard in people with chips on their shoulders, who are often looking for fights or problems. Always ready to point the finger at someone else, they are the perennial victims who always feel that they have been messed over and are seeking someone else to blame.

People with a clipped edge to their voice are often vocally challenging others. What they are saying through their tones is "Just wait! Try to knock this block off my shoulder," or "Just try and say something I don't like, then listen how I will verbally devour you!" Their tones cause an inflamed reaction in others, who often feel they are being challenged for no reason at all. Since their tone may also have a whine to it, these people also may sound as though they are annoyed with you.

This way of speaking has often been referred to in certain social circles as having "attitude," reflecting a nasty disposition. These people are constantly challenging others with their tone of voice and are often engaged in arguments. If someone doesn't agree with them they feel that the other person is wrong. In essence what they are saying through their agitated tone is "Don't even try to challenge me—I know it all! It's either my way or the highway!"

These people have a continuous verbal fire burning within them. When they don't like something, flames are ready at a moment's notice to shoot out of their mouths, burning everyone and everything in their path. The best advice for dealing with such a person with such a tone is to stay as far away as possible to avoid verbal third-degree burns.

15. Choppy, Staccato Tones

A person who speaks in these deliberate tones is usually inflexible, often prissy, self-righteous, and extremely rigid. This type of individual dots every "i" and crosses every "t." They are often headstrong and do not go with the flow. It is often difficult for them to bend or to compromise.

They are reminiscent of the first- or second-grade teacher who speaks to the child in short, simple sentences. Often when you hear this voice pattern, it may take you back to those elementary school days. No adult wants to be spoken to as a child, but unfortunately these choppy, staccato speakers have no clue that their tone is offensive to anyone above the age of five.

This happened to a client of mine, a very successful businessman who came to me for a session. In my waiting room he encountered another of my clients, a gorgeous actress who had arrived early for her appointment. The two of them chatted until I managed to fetch the businessman into my office.

The first thing he said to me after spending time chatting with the actress was, "How sad. What an uptight lady! What a waste to be that stunning and to sound like a prissy, uptight schoolmarm. All she needed was a hair bun and a high-collar dress and she'd fit the role perfectly. When I saw that lady, I immediately thought she was gorgeous, but after hearing her talk, I got put off. I felt like she was talking down to me—like I was beneath her."

This man's assessment of the actress was 100 percent correct. Her voice said it all. Had she known how successful and wonderful this eligible bachelor was maybe her pattern would have changed, but I am glad she revealed her true self before anything occurred. He read her correctly. She was a condescending, uptight, judgmental woman and he knew it just by listening to her overly articulated, choppy, staccato tone.

16. Nasal Whiners with Lockjaw

The lockjaw nasaler is much angrier, more judgmental, and complaining than the nonlockjaw nasaler. While the latter may exhibit a sense of humor, lockjaw nasalers usually don't share that amusement. Instead they seem to have much more pent-up rage.

Award-winning actress Nina Foch says when she coaches an actor or actress for a film, the first question she asks when she sees a tight-locked lower jaw is, "Which parent are you angry at and why?" The performer will often display shock, go into a defensive mode, and deny that there was any problem. Later, they may tearfully admit to it. They may even immediately break down in sobs, letting out years of suppressed anger and emotions harbored against a parent or a toxic person in their life.

The jaw tension results in locked-jaw speaking and a tight nasal pattern that is not considered generous. In fact the person is usually seen as being an uptight, stingy type. This is often an accurate assessment of their personality traits.

17. Sounding Dull and Lifeless

These speakers are perceived as being apathetic, uncaring, aloof, uptight, and repressed. These perceptions are not too far from the truth. Often, these people aren't in touch with their emotions, so they keep an emotional vocal distance from others for fear of getting too close.

This condition may also reflect depression or an inner sadness. These vocally ungenerous people keep others at arm's length because of low self-esteem and the fear of being found out. They are so afraid of having anyone else tap into their emotions that they use noncommittal tones to keep others at bay.

Speaking to one of these unanimated types often induces the tendency to get more animated in order to elicit some type of reaction from them, but this usually doesn't happen. Normally, others become frustrated and disappointed with the lack of feedback.

There might even be a sense of resentment at speaking and finding it is not reciprocated. This is especially true if you have tried repeatedly to communicate with the person to no avail. This can lead to much misunderstanding because it is often so difficult for these speakers to get their message across when there is no subtext of emotion running through their tones. Consequently others cannot read the intricate vocal nuances that give communication its special meaning.

"He's weird. I don't like him. Are you sure he's breathing and he's not really a cadaver? I never know where I stand with him. It's like talking to a wall."

Those were some of the comments John happened to overhear about himself as he was in the men's room. John owned a struggling company. The main problem he had was with personnel. Nobody really liked him and he had no clue why. But this overheard conversation was an eye-opener as he realized that his dull tones were the culprit.

People who speak in dull, lifeless tones generally make others angry. You can't get through to them and they deplete your energy because they don't give you any feedback. Normally a conversation is a give-and-take experience. When you are putting forth the effort to make conversation and you are not getting anything in return, it is extremely frustrating and energy draining.

When you are around these people, you try to become more animated so you can get any kind of reaction. But when this doesn't happen, you tend to feel even more exhausted, rejected, and downright angry.

If someone you know used to speak in animated, lively tones but now uses a dull monotone, rest assured something is wrong. Most likely the person is upset with you or with something in his or her life or is depressed.

There is usually an unwritten, hostile subtext in your communication with a dull, lifeless bore because they produce underlying anger. They tend to be very passive-aggressive people who with-hold a lot of information and are not forthcoming.

Too often there tend to be misunderstandings with people who sound dull and lifeless because they aren't able to convey the true meaning about what they really want to say, so they come across as sneaky and even dishonest.

18. Sounding Sugary Sweet

People with this vocal quality are usually duplicitous, saying one thing and meaning another. Laura was so sugary sweet that she could make you go into a diabetic shock every time she spoke. Her singsong voice oozed forth with gooey tones filled with fawning, creamy words.

She pretended to be a loyal worker at a public relations firm only to stab her coworkers in the back at every opportunity. Others couldn't stand her and complained to the boss. He readily took her side, until he finally saw the writing on the wall. Apparently Laura had undercut her boss by taking away his top client, telling them that she could do the job better and more cheaply. She then left the PR firm and went to work for the prestigious client, who soon saw through her manipulative ways and fired her.

It is difficult to trust anyone who sounds that sweet all the time. The upward-inflected and high-pitched tone signals a person's inner anger. Having seen enough of these people in my practice and having had the unfortunate experience of doing business with them, I can assure you they are definitely angry.

They are passive-aggressive types who will turn on you at a moment's notice. They cannot be trusted because, simply stated, they aren't real. It's not normal always to be that upbeat, happy, and friendly. People have a wide range of emotions and do not just operate on one note, even if it seems to be a pleasant note.

That was the case with Laura, who ended up sweet-toning and sweet-talking the boss to get him on her side. She did minimal work and, while sweetly indicating that she was a loyal employee, was ravaging his business and stealing his most valued contacts.

So whenever you hear that sugary sweetness, keep your ears open—a lot of heat is brewing inside this kettle. Listen for double messages and incongruent behaviors. What you hear is not always what you will experience. Know that trouble is on the way.

19. Pitching the Voice Upward at the End of Sentences

This vocal pattern sounds as though the person is asking a question no matter what they say. Even when telling you their name they sound as though they're asking a question: "Hi. I'm Mary Jones? I'm from Kansas City?" Women more often than men tend to exhibit this vocal tone, which indicates people are tentative and insecure about what they want to say. It screams to the listener that they lack confidence.

I had a client who worked at a company for twelve years. She was always passed over for promotion and wondered why. Finally, someone referred her to me and I clearly knew why. Even though she knew her company inside and out and what would be expected in her new job, she sounded as though it was her first day. Practically every sentence that came out of her mouth sounded as though she was asking permission or a question. As we spoke, she suddenly revealed she wasn't really that sure about whether she could handle all the responsibility and the long hours. She loved the company and certainly wanted more money but she didn't know if she was ready to move up.

She was a single parent with growing kids at home, and it would be more responsibility and would present a daunting challenge. Her rising tone at the end of sentences and her questioning inflection clearly reflected her self-doubts concerning her job.

Once we addressed esteem issues during our sessions, her vocal pitch changed dramatically. It became lower, which reflected more self-confidence. She no longer spoke in her questioning up-pitched tone. She felt more confident to take on the job, accept the greater responsibility, and hire help for her kids.

Not all people who speak in upwardly pitched sentences are insecure or suffer from low self-esteem. They may have just developed a habit of talking in "uptalk," a tone typically used by many teens and young adults so they fit in with their peer group. There is nothing wrong with that. It is like speaking a cool foreign language that gives young people a feeling of belonging. But if it's spoken outside the peer group, there can be a problem.

If you are a parent, please don't encourage your kids to use this uptalk at home or in school. If they get into a habit and use it in the real world, it can be devastating in terms of how adults perceive them. This could affect their future in the job market and in business.

20. Sounding Too Slow and Deliberate

Like those who speak too fast, the too-slow speaker is often not conscious of the feelings of others because they suffer from poor self-esteem. They may be slow and deliberate because they don't want to make any errors; however, they may actually be pompous and arrogant, overarticulating their words and sounds to make sure others receive all the information they dole out.

Even though they may see you get bored and roll your eyes, they will often ignore you and continue droning on. They are blocking you out. Selfish and consumed with getting their message across, they are not paying attention to you or to your body or facial cues. In a way, it is a power trip—an aggressively rude mode to ignore human interaction, an overtly hostile act.

These people tend to have internal sadness and are self-absorbed. Studies on emotion and speech have associated sadness with slow speech.

It's important not to mistake this speech pattern for the one used by Southerners, who speak more slowly than people from other regions because they spend more time drawing out their vowels. You will know the difference based upon how annoying it feels to you and how uncomfortable it makes you feel when you are ignored and when a person is not paying attention to you.

It is also important not to attribute this deliberate speech pattern to someone with a neuromotor condition whose speech slows the person down, nor to someone who may speak more slowly as a side effect of taking certain medications.

Making Your Voice Give the Right Message

Although your tone mirrors your personality, there are many instances where the voice produces the wrong message. You may not possess these negative characteristics at all. But the fact that you have a particular voice quality may still give people a negative impression.

In order to remedy the problem of being mislabeled and being misinterpreted, it is in your best interest to read my book *Talk to Win,* or get one of my audiotapes. You may also contact me for a personal consultation by referring to Appendix C of this book.

You can learn to project your voice at the right pitch, and establish rich and clear resonant tones. You will also learn to become more enthusiastic and emotionally connected when you communicate so people will perceive you in a powerful and exciting way. This translates into how well you do in both your business and your social life.

Now that you've learned about the vocal code, let's move on to the code of body language.

CHAPTER 7

Understanding the Body Language Code

The body language code is a combination of movements, gestures, and mannerisms that communicate specific messages in various circumstances and situations. If you listen carefully to people and watch their body and facial movements, you will learn plenty. You will learn whether they are lying or telling the truth; whether they like you or not. You will learn if they meant what they said and said what they meant.

In this chapter, I will help you to learn what some of these movements are and what certain movements, postures, and nuances really mean.

Body Language Code Survey

In order to determine what a person is really communicating through body language, it is essential for you to examine several

components of how a person moves and how they present themselves.

1. Does the person lean toward you when speaking or listening?
2. Does the person back or lean away from you when speaking or listening?
3. Does the person invade your space?
4. Does the person keep his or her distance from you, or stand too far away?
5. Does the person keep a comfortable distance from you?
6. Are the arms crossed?
7. Does the person fidget?
8. Does the person rock back and forth?
9. Does the person tap the feet?
10. Does the person tap the fingers?
11. Is the posture stiff and rigid?
12. Is the posture too relaxed or sloppy?
13. Is the posture comfortable and relaxed?
14. Does the person mirror (copy) your body language?
15. Does the person slump over?
16. Does the person lunge forward?
17. Does the person appear to be posing?
18. Does the person exhibit little movement?
19. Is the posture open and welcoming?
20. Is the posture closed and withdrawn?
21. Are the head and body turned away from you?
22. Does the person support the head with the hand when speaking or listening?
23. Does the person lean forward when listening?
24. Do they stand on one foot?
25. Is the tie or collar loosened?
26. Is the head tipped to the side when listening?
27. Does the person jerk the head away from the person to whom he or she is speaking?

28. Is the head bowed or lowered?
29. Does the person thrust the head forward from the shoulders?
30. Is the head tossed backward?
31. Does the person scratch the head, especially at the crown region?
32. Do they sweat a lot?
33. Does the person shrug their shoulders?
34. Are the arms akimbo?
35. Are the arms open?
36. Does the person gesture wildly?
37. Does the person use the arms minimally while speaking?
38. Does the person touch himself or herself when speaking?
39. Does the person gesture toward his or her body?
40. Does the person pinch or rub the nose when speaking?
41. Does the person rub the eyes?
42. Does the person rub the neck?
43. Does the person tend to hide the hands when speaking?
44. Are the fists clenched?
45. Are the hand movements staccato and jerky?
46. Does the person point the finger outward when speaking?
47. Does the person keep the hands folded?
48. Does the person clasp the hands together tightly?
49. Are the palms of the hands exposed?
50. Does the person use the hands minimally when speaking?
51. Is there excessive hand movement?
52. Does the person fiddle with jewelry or play with the hair?
53. Does the person bite the nails or pick at the fingers and hands?
54. Does the person twiddle the thumbs or move the fingers repetitively?
55. Are the hand movements strong and deliberate?
56. Does the person steeple or touch the fingertips together when speaking?
57. Does the person touch you a lot?

58. Does the person never touch you?
59. Does the person have a hard or overly strong touch?
60. Does the person have a firm handshake?
61. Does the person have an overly strong handshake?
62. Does the person have a weak handshake?
63. Are the feet firmly planted on the ground?
64. Do the feet face you directly when the person is sitting or standing?
65. Does the person jiggle the feet when listening or talking?
66. Does the person wrap one foot around the other?
67. Does the person lock the ankles when sitting?
68. Are the legs apart when sitting?
69. Are the legs crossed?
70. Is one knee crossed directly over the other knee?
71. Does the person slap the thighs in a repeated motion?
72. Does the person sit with one leg under another?
73. Are the legs outstretched, widely apart?
74. Does the person stand on one leg?
75. Does the person walk at a slow pace?
76. Does the person look down when walking?
77. Does the person walk with a raised chin, swinging the arms in an exaggerated manner?
78. Does the person walk at a deliberate, fixed pace?
79. Does the person walk timidly, as though walking on egg-shells?
80. Does the person walk on the tiptoes?
81. Does the person walk at a clipped and rapid pace?
82. Does the person have mechanical, rigid arm movements and take short steps?
83. Does the person have a slight bounce to the walk as they hold the head up and swing the arms in a relaxed and easy manner?
84. Does the person wear outdated clothes?
85. Are the clothes unkempt or sloppy?

86. Does the person wear the latest fashions?
87. Does the person dress in a sexy and revealing manner?
88. Does the person wear loud colors and bold patterns?
89. Does the person wear dull and boring styles and colors?
90. Does the person dress conservatively?
91. Is the person overly buttoned and creased?
92. Is the person dressed inappropriately for the occasion?
93. Is the person dressed tastefully and appropriately for the occasion?
94. Is the person unkempt and unhygienic?
95. Is the hair well groomed?
96. Is the hair in style?
97. Does the person change the hair style and color often?
98. Does the person wear a hairpiece or try to comb the hair over to the side if balding?
99. Is the person overly meticulous about grooming?
100. Does the person wear too much or too little makeup?

As you read this chapter, you will discover what these indicators mean and how they relate to a person's personality profile.

Celebrity Body Reading

Senator John McCain held a press conference with then governor George W. Bush, saying he would endorse Governor Bush in his run for the presidency. Even though his words said one thing, his body language said another. It reflected the hurtful feelings and bitterness Senator McCain still harbored toward Governor Bush after the nasty campaign. The media sensed this and continually reported that McCain's body language was inconsistent with his words. They saw the tension and stiffness when he was in Bush's presence. They did not see the relaxed person they usually observed. The media reaction was not uncommon. Because we see world events as they take place, we have become media savvy.

Several years ago, I did an article for *Cosmopolitan* magazine where I analyzed a series of candid photographs of celebrity couples to determine which of the couples would stay together, based upon their body language in the photos. The pictures were of actors Jim Carrey and Lauren Holly, Brooke Shields and tennis player Andrei Agassi, Pamela Anderson and musician husband Tommy Lee. Here is what I observed:

Lauren Holly was holding Jim Carrey's hand, literally hanging onto the relationship for dear life. There was a lot of muscle tension in her arms and hands as she grabbed onto her husband. In practically all the photos Jim Carrey was looking away from Lauren, toward the camera and at his fans. There didn't seem to be a togetherness between them. In fact, Carrey never leaned his body toward her. There was a stiffness and what appeared to be physical tension between them. So I wasn't surprised when the two split up.

There was also a visible body stiffness and tension between Andrei Agassi and Brooke Shields. This stands in sharp contrast to the photos of Agassi and his new love, tennis player Steffi Graf. Each appears relaxed, with their bodies leaning toward each other, indicating the strong comfort level they feel.

Initially, Pamela Anderson and Tommy Lee couldn't get enough of each another. They were always pictured chest to chest, pelvis to pelvis. My concern in observing photos of when they first got together was whether anything would be left when the temperature of their heated relationship inevitably dropped. Obviously not, because after a tumultuous and often violent relationship, they have split for the second time, perhaps for good.

The next time you look at the supermarket tabloids, study them carefully, but with a different point of view. Study people's body movement and posture. What you observe will tell you volumes about how people really feel toward one another.

See how far apart the couple stands. Observe the placement of their hands, arms, and legs. Do they lean into each other? Are they tense or relaxed? Do they stand side by side, or is one in front of the other? If you look carefully, you will find a lot of information. You will discover what you read and heard isn't necessarily true. Even though the celebrity couple or their spokesperson has made assurances everything is fine, you may find the opposite is true.

Former talk show hostess Kathie Lee Gifford's insistence that she forgave husband Frank Gifford for cheating on her read quite differently. As she sat next to Frank during an interview with Diane Sawyer, one could see her tight jaw, her pursed lips, and her chin jutting forward in a hostile position. Then there were the harsh tones in her vocal code, which were in great contrast to the sweet and forgiving words she wanted the public to believe.

Frank's words clashed with his body language. He refused to look at Kathie Lee, sat emotionless, and would not return her loving gesture of a hand placed over his. His message was, "I am angry and have had enough of Kathie Lee making me 'pay' for my indiscretion by humiliating and publicly punishing me!"

The Body Doesn't Lie

The body tells you a great deal about yourself and others. Gestures, posture, and body position mean something because these signals are the body's attempt to bring suppressed feelings to the surface. In fact, studies show that whenever you attempt to hide your emotions, your blood pressure rises.

As we learned in the last chapter, every gesture and movement sends a clear message of how you are feeling, whether you know it or not. Body language can reinforce or contradict verbal messages because a person's body discloses *true* feelings.

Former President Nixon showed how he felt through his body language. He showed others he wasn't comfortable when he was asked a difficult question. He would swivel his head and body away from anyone who would ask such a question. He was simply distancing himself from the questioner, which made him appear untrustworthy. By merely observing his body language people knew something wasn't right. They knew that he had something to hide.

Several years ago, I was treating Marissa, a fifteen-year-old who impressed me immensely. Throughout our sessions, I was struck not only by her intelligence, but also by her excellent posture and deliberate hand and arm movements. This was evidence of a positive sense of self-confidence.

All of that changed, however, when her mother attended a session with her. It was as though Marissa had turned into a different person. Her demeanor metamorphosed. Her head dropped toward her chest and she couldn't make eye contact with her mother or with me. She sat with her hands folded politely on her lap.

I felt for Marissa because I knew exactly what was happening. She was being influenced by a bullying mother whose presence dwarfed her. Marissa was obviously intimidated and, in trying to acquiesce to her mother's power, Marissa was sacrificing a large part of her self-confidence.

When I brought this to both their attention, Marissa finally acknowledged she always felt uncomfortable around her mother. She could never meet her mother's expectations, let alone please her. Now that she understood, the channels of communication opened and mother and daughter could finally learn to treat one another with the respect they both deserved.

Leaning

When you like a person, you tend to lean toward them. It is a sign you are interested in the person and what they have to say. When you are extremely interested, the body will lean forward while the legs tend to be drawn back. When a person leans sideways while seated, it means they are exhibiting friendliness toward you. When you don't like a person, feel bored around them, or don't feel comfortable, you tend to lean backward.

I once had lunch with a female friend who was interested in dating one of the men in our party. After he excused himself to go to the men's room, my friend gushed like a school girl and asked if I thought she had a chance with him. I didn't want to be the one to burst her bubble, so I told her how to find out for herself. I told her to see how close he got and if he leaned toward her.

The man soon returned and my friend quickly got her answer. It was somewhere between slim and none. The man was leaning back in his chair. When she reached over to touch him, he would recoil in discomfort. He was stiff and very formal when speaking to her and didn't pay much attention. The man was spoken for. He was in a committed relationship with someone else and wasn't interested. He let her know through his body language.

Zone Stepping

Just as animals have rules for space and territoriality, so do humans. When an animal invades another animal's space, the animal feels threatened and may attack. The same holds true for humans. Each culture has rules that dictate how close or far one person must sit or stand from another. Latin and Middle Eastern people stand closer together than Westerners, who aren't used to someone invading their space. But if you are a Westerner visiting another culture, it is a good idea to become familiar with—and employ—the local customs.

No matter the culture, people who overstep space boundaries are either power-playing, narcissistic types or are completely unaware of what they are doing. When someone gets very close and starts talking to you, you may act negatively or rebel. You might retreat and withdraw until you excuse yourself completely. You may find yourself crossing your arms (a subconscious way of protecting yourself), pulling back your face, or even tucking your chin into your chest. You might begin tapping your foot, fidgeting, or shifting your posture. You may also notice that your voice becomes tense and you tell the person to back off.

Studies have been done where experimenters have purposely occupied another person's space, making it too close for comfort. The other person usually recoils to display their discomfort level.

People will often purposely stand too close because it makes the other person feel self-conscious. Jumping into one's territory threatens the person whose space is being invaded. They may shrink back, wondering about your intentions. Standing too close offends most people. No matter what is said, they cannot shake the negative feelings they may feel toward you.

Finally, moving too close may make someone defensive and self-conscious about personal hygiene, such as breath or body odor. Or the person may be repelled by your body odor and breath. On the other hand, if someone you like invades your space, there may be no negative effect, because you are welcoming the person into your space.

It is important to note that a person who feels powerful and confident usually takes up more physical space, extending the arms and legs and generally taking up more room. Conversely, a less-secure person tends to pull the arms and legs toward themselves, retreating into a type of fetal position.

Standing Too Far Away

People who stand too far away are perceived as being arrogant, snobby, or feeling as though they are better than you. They literally don't want to get too close. They may be sitting or standing far away because they don't like you. You may offend them by who you are, what you say, how you smell, or how you look. Often people who distance themselves physically from others feel threatened.

Mirroring Movements

If you want to tell if someone is attracted to you, see if they follow your movements. If either of you copies the other's body language gestures (crossing legs in unison, placing hands under the chin, clasping fingers, and the like) chances are either or both of you are relating to the other person. Mirroring another person says one wants to be like the other person.

Rocking Back and Forth

This behavior signals that a person is impatient or anxious. Adults rock back and forth when they are uncomfortable, to calm themselves during anxious moments.

It is not uncommon to see this behavior with children, especially those with autism. This is a self-stimulating behavior to relieve anxiety.

When adults exhibit this behavior it makes others uncomfortable because they are distracted by it. It makes them lose their focus and concentration on what the person who is rocking back and forth is trying to say.

Fidgeting

When people move restlessly, they are telling you a number of things. They may be feeling nervous, signaling they don't want to be there. They may engage in hand wringing or foot tapping, which says they are anxious and may also be irritated. When a person is uncomfortable they may move about in order to feel more comfortable.

When people feel uncomfortable, their body temperature rises slightly, and they literally begin to feel hotter and more uncomfortable. They may truly be feeling "hot under the collar" and may fidget with their tie in an attempt to loosen it.

So when you see someone fidgeting, the person is sending a message that he or she feels uncomfortable or anxious about something. Perhaps they haven't told the truth, or they want to leave their environment.

Head Tilting

Tipping the head to one side signifies that someone is interested and is listening to what you have to say. You have their full attention and they are concentrating on what you are saying.

You may notice that little children who haven't learned to speak yet frequently exhibit this head tilting behavior when you are speaking to them. It indicates that they are attentive and are listening to you.

Head Jerking

People listening to something that doesn't please them will tend to jerk the head away from the other person. It seems to be an automatic response to create a barrier between the person and the source of discomfort.

Head Nodding

People who constantly nod the head yes while you are speaking may be pleasers, whose aim is to make you feel comfortable. They tend to have a deep-rooted desire to be liked. The head nodding is saying, "Like me—I agree with everything you say, so like me back." They are often insecure people who fear rejection.

When someone sways the head or rocks it from side to side, it may mean the person is expressing doubt or reluctance over what has been said. The head may be moving from side to side as a means of weighing what was said and what position the person will take in response.

Head Bowing

Unless you are in a religious ceremony or from a culture where bowing one's head is a sign of respect, communication with a bowed head screams that such people are unsure of themselves. They may also be unhappy or depressed, with low self-esteem.

As mentioned earlier, the late Princess Diana used to bow her head when she spoke. Early on it may have been a submissive gesture, but later she continued to speak with head bowed, which reflected her state of unhappiness and may have indicated an insecurity in her role as princess.

Forward Head Thrusting

The head thrust forward signals an impending threat. Much like jutting the chin, it is an aggressive movement that indicates the person is ready to take an aggressive or even hostile approach to the problem at hand.

When a person shakes the head or tosses it back, this movement tends to express disdain or arrogance.

Head Scratching

Unless someone has lice or a scalp infection, head scratching means the person is feeling confusion or isn't sure of something.

One evening, I was working with my music producer on a song I had written. I noticed he suddenly began to scratch the crown of his head in a vigorous manner. "You're not sure about the conclusion of the song are you?" I asked.

"You're right," he replied. "I want to try something different and a bit more dramatic at the end of the song." By observing him scratch his head, I learned he was not exactly sure where to go. He knew he wanted to do something different at the end of my song, yet he was concerned he might offend me by changing an aspect of the song.

Here's another example. Let's say when you ask a question someone scratches his or her head. The person is telling you that he or she is unsure of the question or of what answer to give. Therefore, it is in everyone's best interest if you ask the question again in a different way so the person will fully understand what you want. Rephrasing a question in a different manner also gives the person time to come up with an answer.

Shoulder Shrugging

When people shrug their shoulders, it may mean they are not telling the truth, are not being forthright, or are feeling indifferent. They may also be saying, "I don't know," "I'm not sure," or "I don't believe you."

People who are lying tend to exhibit this shoulder shrug very quickly. In this case it is not deliberate and means something entirely different from not caring or being indifferent. What they are saying is, "I am not telling the truth." This quick shrug is an unconscious attempt at appearing cool, calm, and collected, but in reality they may not be.

If a person raises the shoulders and does not create a shrug, but keeps them in that raised position, it says, "I am harmless." Marilyn Monroe often used this gesture to indicate her sexiness and approachability.

Posturing: Straight and Not

Posture reflects how people feel about others as well as about themselves. Someone with confident posture has the back straight, shoulders rolled back, head erect, buttocks tight. The person stands with comfort and ease, the weight evenly distributed onto the legs. If the person is sitting, both the legs and arms are uncrossed in an open position.

People with confident posture tend to feel as comfortable hanging out at a mall with friends as at black tie affairs. They use hands and arms animatedly to illustrate their points. They tend to focus on others. As a result, they lose awareness of how they are performing and become more aware of others. They tend to be open and secure, traits that make them more attractive to others. An open and relaxed posture makes others feel good.

On the other hand, different postures indicate other emotions.

1. Slumped-over Posture

When someone is sad, they tend to slump. Rounded shoulders is a look of resignation, a sign of low self-confidence or even depression. It is says this person is shouldering a burden. Someone who consistently maintains this posture may withdraw from a situation or from life in general. It may also mean that the person is uninterested in you or what you have to say. The person does not lunge forward, but retreats—the flight manifestation of the fight or flight response.

Usually when a person has rounded shoulders and a slumping posture, there are collapsed chest areas as well. Because inner organs are also depressed, they can't provide the support necessary to enable the person to properly project vocally.

2. Lunging Forward Posture

When the body lunges forward with the neck extended, you can be sure the person is angry. The jaw may jut forward and the fists may also be clenched. There will also appear to be a great deal of muscle tension. This is a fight response. You can quickly tell that when someone is in a hurry and walks with their body lunging forward, they are angry.

3. Rigid Posture

People with rigid, military-like posture are often uptight and inflexible in their decisions and point of view. They tend to see things as black or white and often have the "my way or the highway" attitude, making them authoritarian in nature.

They may often have a snobbish air about them, an "I'm better than you" attitude. With the head lifted, they typically look down at people. They appreciate neatness and orderliness and have a difficult time functioning outside familiar parameters.

4. Poser Posture

These people have a contrived posture that looks as if they are posing and are always conscious of others looking at them. They are the type who would give you a kiss on both cheeks, only to turn around to see who was watching their act. They will stand near a bar, trying to look cool, hip, and part of the scene.

Although they may appear snobby and seem to have an attitude, they are really insecure, self-conscious, and self-absorbed. They have a narcissistic view that life revolves around them.

5. Closed Posture

People who do not like you or who disagree with what you have said will often do a number of things, body-wise. They primarily have closed postures where they hold the head and trunk erect, while at the same time crossing the arms over the chest. If they are in a sitting position, they may cross the legs above the knee.

6. Neutral Posture

People who have not formed an opinion about you or have not made up their mind about a situation often fold their hands in front of them if they are standing. If they are seated, they usually fold their hands on their lap and will cross their legs above the knee in a wait-and-see attitude. They are partly in an open position, with their head and torso in an upright position and with open arms, and partly in a closed position, with their hands on their lap, without fingers interlocking and with legs tightly crossed above the knee.

7. Bored Posture

When bored or uninterested, people will turn their heads and eventually their bodies from you. If they have been leaning forward they will often lean back. If they are sitting, their legs will straighten after being drawn back and the trunk of the body will assume a more erect position.

The fingers will be interlocked and the hands will rest in the lap. If they become even less interested, the head will lean and will often require the support of the hand.

The body in the bored posture usually has a backward lean with the legs outstretched. If the person is standing, the hands may be in front, with fingers interlocked and the head turned away from the other person.

Be Fully Armed

The way in which someone uses the arms tells you a great deal about how the person is feeling emotionally. I will explain various arm positions, which will give you some insight about what a person's arms are telling you.

1. Arms Crossed

This is a defensive gesture exhibited when someone feels uncomfortable and wants to protect himself or herself. It may also mean the person is closing off to you. When a person doesn't feel secure, he or she tries to take up less physical space.

Unless the temperature in the room is cold and people have crossed their arms to stay warm, those who fold their arms across their chest say they are holding onto their position, bracing themselves, which means they are closed off to any position you may offer. This stance is also accompanied by nervousness and tension. Crossing the arms over the body practically screams that someone has something to hide. So when you see someone with arms folded across the chest, it means the person is withdrawing. Often, women who have large breasts or who do not feel comfortable about their bodies engage in this position.

2. Arms Akimbo

When the arms are placed on the hips and the elbows protrude from the sides of the body, it means "Stay away from me" or "Don't mess with me." It is, as anthropologist Desmond Morris says, "an anti-embrace posture." It is also a display of extreme confidence and independence.

In a social situation when one person wants to exclude another from a group, he or she may send a message by placing a single arm on a hip. I once noticed this behavior at a party. A woman was very possessive over her new, highly attractive boyfriend. Every time another woman came up and started to speak to him, she attempted to elbow her with her right arm, which was strategically placed on her hip. She would rapidly swing around so it would block the other woman from reaching him, while she would accidentally on purpose strike the woman with her elbow. She was telling the woman in no uncertain terms to keep her distance from her beau.

3. Open Arms

Clasping the arms behind the back shows openness; people in this posture signal that they feel no need to protect themselves. On walkabouts where they meet with their subjects, the British Royal family often display this stance, torso exposed and arms at bay, indicating they are at ease.

This position presents a show of confidence. Soldiers often assume this stance with their arms clasped behind their backs when they are ordered to stand at ease. They are relaxed, open, and have nothing to hide.

4. Arms Flailing

In many Mediterranean and Middle Eastern cultures, arm flailing is often employed to express certain points during a conversation, as part of normal communication. But arms flailing in Western cultures may mean something completely different: that a person is out of control, highly emotional, or extremely angry.

Emotional Hands

How someone holds the hands can tell you a lot about the person's emotional state. Here are what some of these hand gestures mean.

1. Hidden Hands

When a person hides the hands while speaking—such as putting them in the pockets—he or she may be hiding valuable information, not wanting to reveal something personally important. I once saw my friend Marty at an event and asked him how his wife, Jeanie, was doing. "Oh, she's doing great," he replied, as he placed his hand in his pocket and immediately changed the subject. I found out several days later that he and Jeanie were having marital problems and were headed toward divorce.

2. Angry Hands

Clenching the fist tends to mean that a person is not revealing his or her emotions verbally. Whenever you see a clenched hand while someone is speaking, the person is truly angry or upset. If the clenched fist hides the thumb, the person is usually feeling threatened, intimidated, or worried. Holding onto the thumbs in a fist-like position is a protective device, much like crossing of the arms. Pointing outward with the pointer finger or employing staccato and jerky hand movements when speaking also signifies someone is harboring anger.

3. Lying Hands

A person who is not being forthright is usually less expressive with the hands, which may be clenched, made into a fist, or kept folded or in the pockets. Notice how tightly a person has the hands clasped while talking: the tighter, the more tense someone is.

When a person is clutching something, such as a chair, it is as though he or she is trying to hold onto reality. People who are holding onto themselves are tense or insecure and are literally trying to get a grip. In so doing, they may be engaging in a lie or attempting to avoid experiencing powerful emotions.

4. Honest Hands

Conversely, when a person is being truthful, the palms of the hands will be exposed and the fingers will usually be extended. This shows an openness and an interest in others. It is an accepting gesture and means the person is receptive and welcoming of you and your ideas. Showing the palm is also a sign that makes you more vulnerable to another person. On the other hand, a person who shows you the back of the hand is usually not being as receptive and open, but is closed off.

5. Expressively Charged Hands

When people are expressive and highly emotional about something they believe, they will wave their hands and arms around to show their passion. If they don't believe in something, their arms and hands won't move as much.

6. Stubborn Hands

When you notice a stiff thumb with the fingers straight or forming a fist, it means the person is firmly planted in their position and won't move from it. You will have hard time bringing a person making this gesture to your point of view.

7. Impatient Hands

Drumming fingers or tapping them on a desk or table usually indicates impatience or nervousness. Similarly, fiddling with objects like a necklace or bracelet or playing with the hair shows insecurity, tension, and nervousness. It says the person is unsure and needs to touch something tangible to feel comfortable.

8. Pressured Hands

Nail mutilation, biting or picking at cuticles, hand wringing, and fidgeting also indicate anxiousness. These unconscious gestures are what people do when they feel pressured, even though the inner turmoil may not be apparent in the person's conversation. These gestures may also be a sign of anger and frustration.

9. Bored Hands

Someone who is feeling frustrated or bored may twiddle the thumbs, with the fingers interlocked and the thumbs rotating around each other. This physical action is an attempt to relieve boredom.

10. Comfortable Hands

When a person is comfortable, it is reflected in the hands. Hand movements are strong and deliberate, yet flowing and unmechanical. A person who clasps the hands behind their head, with arms akimbo, is demonstrating a sense of security, signifying feelings of comfort and ease.

11. Confident Hands

A self-assured person often exhibits numerous hand gestures that reflect confidence. Steepling (touching the fingertips of each hand together to form a steeple) is a self-assured gesture often used by teachers, ministers, politicians, lawyers, and those responsible for disseminating information. People who negotiate also use this gesture.

Touching

Everyone needs to be touched, as anthropologist Ashley Montagu points out in his book, *Touching*. A slight touch on the back, shoulder, arm, or hand conveys emotional support from a warm person. Touching a person while talking is also useful because it can help direct the person's attention to an important point you are making.

Those who engage in excessive touching may be telling you a great deal about their feelings about you and themselves. It may be a sign of jealousy and control, in which case it may be a hostile act I call *invasive touching*. There are also people who touch a lot because they have a strong need to be liked and accepted.

Joe, a fifty-three-year-old photographer, was always touching people after meeting them. He would good-naturedly put his arms on the backs of men or touch a woman's arm as he told them a story. Because Joe was extremely insecure, he wanted to make sure he had people's attention at all times. So he reassured himself by touching the person, who would inevitably perk up and respond positively.

Some people are not as warm and touchy-feely as Joe. Some people touch others as a power play; they are being condescending to the person they are touching. Others may use touch to feel a sense of control or one-upmanship—especially if they are feeling jealous, insecure, or threatened by you. These people may use touch as a power trip. One of the best ways to regain your power is to tell the excessive toucher you prefer not to be touched.

Self-Touching

When someone frequently touches the face, he or she is not necessarily telling the truth. The person may be feeling uncomfortable and may not be completely forthright. In moving the hands toward the mouth or eyes immediately after telling a lie, a person creates a barrier between the self and the listener.

Unless someone has a cold or allergies, pinching or squeezing the nose indicates that a person is uncomfortable in a particular situation. Let's say you ask a man to help you move a heavy chair. Just before he answers yes, his hand moves up to his nose. This gesture indicates that he doesn't really feel like moving the chair. This is similar to what happens when someone touches or covers the mouth after telling you something, which often means the person is not being truthful or isn't happy about what you said.

Rubbing the eyes means a person has had enough and is signaling you to stop doing what you are doing. Rubbing the back of the neck often means someone is feeling uncomfortable and is perhaps lying, storing repressed thoughts about what is true.

Nontouchers

People who don't touch are usually stiff and uptight people with a great deal of insecurity. They may have a lot of neurotic habits and are often afraid of others. They are not comfortable with themselves or with others. They are usually loners and are often self-consumed and selfish. Sometimes, people who don't like to be touched have suffered emotional or physical abuse as children and their lack of touching may be a reaction to childhood experiences.

Hard Touchers

When someone's touch is so hard that it hurts when they touch or grab onto you, that person is expressing competitiveness or inner rage toward you. You need to let such people know that their touch is uncomfortable and unwelcome. Keep your distance.

Handshakes

The way a person shakes your hand speaks volumes. Someone who employs a comfortable yet firm grip conveys a message of confidence; that person is open and has nothing to hide. Strong handshakes are often associated with strong character, while a weak handshake is usually associated with weak character.

If someone attempts to shake your hand by grabbing the tip of your fingers or by offering a weak or awkward, fishlike handshake, that says the person can't connect with you. He or she may feel intimidated or insecure and isn't able to relate.

Often, men aren't sure how to shake a woman's hand. In an attempt to appear gentlemanly, they may dole out a timid handshake. This reflects a lack of strength. On the other hand, a crushing, forceful, pain-producing handshake says the person is aggressive, hostile, and is attempting to assert dominance.

Hand Talking

You can tell a great deal by the way a person uses the hands when speaking. The use of the hands during conversation is a means of punctuating speech, a way of emphasizing certain points, changing a topic, or stopping the conversation. A change in the position of the hand, pointing, touching, or even holding up the hand, all indicate certain meanings.

Hands also tell a great deal about a person's emotional state. A person who is conversing calmly yet speaks with a clenched fist may not be honest. This may be a sign of anger at what you said, or even an indication that the person dislikes you.

Emotional Feet

Just as people's hands and arms tell you a great deal about them emotionally, so does the position of their feet and legs. Feet are one of the most honest body parts; they truly reflect how a person feels and thinks. While it is possible to control one's facial expression, posture, and hand movements, it is extremely difficult to control one's feet.

1. Honest Feet

If a person's feet are together, planted firmly on the ground, facing you directly, chances are the person is forthright, open, and balanced.

On the other hand, if the foot is resting on its outward edge or on the heel, the person may actually be a heel and may very well not be telling the truth.

2. Foot Jiggling

When someone jiggles or taps the foot, he or she is expressing impatience or boredom. The foot jiggle and tap are running-away actions, where the person is literally saying, "I don't want to be here."

3. Foot Locking

A foot lock (wrapping one foot around the leg) is an unconscious tell-tale sign that a person is feeling nervous or uncomfortable. No matter how relaxed the upper body is, that foot position is a sign of nervousness.

4. Ankle Locking

Someone is usually holding something back when he or she locks the ankles by placing one ankle over the other. The person may be holding back an emotion or information, bracing so as not to reveal pertinent information.

This gesture also indicates tension. Often, people who need to go to the bathroom do this gesture as a means of literally holding themselves back. It is also not uncommon to see this gesture among passengers who are nervous or uncomfortable during airplane takeoffs.

Leg Reading

How people position their legs reveals a great deal about them. Leg placement and location can help determine whether a person is being honest and confident or ambitious or insecure.

1. Confident Legs

Legs that are apart when a person sits signal openness and confidence. When a woman is wearing a skirt, the legs will be less apart for obvious reasons. If the legs are together and closed at the knees, it indicates an openness and sense of self-assuredness. If both feet are on the ground and pointing toward the other person with the knees together, it demonstrates frankness and honesty. Confidence and self-assuredness in both men and women are apparent if the legs are crossed, but only if one knee is crossed directly over the other.

2. Lying Legs

When one leg is crossed above the knee, the person is grounding or bracing themselves. This means they may not be confident or may not be telling the truth about something.

3. Get-Me-out-of-Here Legs

Let's say you are speaking to someone who is facing you and looking at you, with head and torso in your direction. But you happen to glance downward and notice that the person's legs and feet are pointed in the opposite direction. What you have observed is that this person wants to leave and doesn't really want to talk to you. When a person is uncomfortable with you, their legs literally move toward the door to escape.

Another gesture that indicates a person wants to leave is slapping the thighs in a repeated and rhythmic motion. You will often see a person slapping the outside of the thighs, which indicates the person wants to go but can't. It is similar to a tapping of the foot, which may indicate a wish to depart but fear of being impolite.

4. Independent Legs

Someone who sits with one leg under the other is usually an independent, free-spirited, informal type of person, or else is unaware of proper sitting positions. This type of person may not be concerned about what others think.

5. Dominant Legs

Legs stretched out in front of someone, whether crossed or not, show the person is being dominant. Those who sit in this manner may be strong-willed people who may exhibit bullyish behavior.

There appears to be a self-centered manner in their attempt to be noticed.

6. One-Legged Stance

Unless you have a physical challenge, standing on one leg is highly distracting. Others may perceive you as being uncomfortable or in pain. Subconsciously, the person to whom you are speaking tends to be more concerned about how you are feeling than what you are saying.

Standing on one leg is usually a habit. People are often unaware how they come across to others and may do it routinely. This stance may offend others and doesn't elicit a great deal of trust and confidence.

The Walk

People usually have a characteristic walk that is recognizable to those who are familiar with the person. You may see someone walking toward you from a great distance, not see his or her features, and still know it is a friend or family member. Now we will examine how a person's walk reflects their emotional state.

1. The Depressed Walk

When a person is feeling down in the dumps, the head will be bowed, the shoulders will be stooped, and the person will rarely look up at where he or she is going. The eyes usually look down and the pace is often lethargic.

2. The "I'm All That!" Walk

People who think they are better than others usually walk with their chins raised and swing their arms in an exaggerated manner. They rarely look at others; they assume everyone is watching them. Their posture is upright to the point of being rigid and their chests often protrude. Their legs tend to be rigid and they walk in a deliberate, fixed pace. They often make a lot of noise when they walk so you usually hear their footsteps.

3. The Timid Walk

Someone who is timid or is unsure of others' feelings tends to walk on tiptoes. The person will often be slightly hunched over and noninvasive. You may not hear the person coming into the room, he or she is so quiet. The pace is tentative, not deliberate.

4. The Uptight Walk

An uptight and rigid person usually has an uptight and rigid walk that mirrors the personality. Such a person walks in a clipped, rapidly paced way, often taking short steps and demonstrating rigid arm movements that appear to be mechanical.

5. The Confident Walk

Confident individuals have an evenly paced gait that seems to have a slight happy bounce. They look at people when they walk and often smile. Their posture is straight with the head up, and the arms swing at their sides in an easy and relaxed manner.

What You Wear

In addition to reading people's posture and body movements, you can learn a lot about them from the way they dress, too.

1. Outdated Clothes

If a person wears clothing that is outdated, worn, ill-fitting, or out of style, it may indicate they cannot afford new clothes or are simply not with the times.

2. Unkempt Clothes

If a person's clothing is sloppy, stained, smelly, or unkempt, it tells you they have low self-esteem or are not tuned into themselves.

3. High-Fashion Clothes

People who wear the latest fashion or follow the latest fads are often highly concerned what others think. They may have a strong desire to fit in and feel insecure if they don't have trendy clothes to hide behind.

4. Sexy Clothes

People who wear ultra-sexy and revealing clothes are looking for attention. This is typical Hollywood attire, where many men and women come to be noticed and discovered. The sexier and more outrageous the clothing, the more likelihood of drawing attention. Dressing in revealing clothing may be fine for people seeking sexual attention, but those who dress like that on a regular basis are usually sexually and emotionally insecure and are trying to compensate for feelings of inadequacy.

5. Loud Clothes

People who wear loud colors and clothes and accessories that scream "notice me!" also tend to be insecure. They have a strong need for attention that is often tied into a low sense of self-esteem. On the other hand, a flash of color is a good thing. It shows that the person is happy, upbeat, and in a good mood. It also suggests creativity.

6. Boring Clothes

By contrast, people who wear boring colors and conservative styles usually do not want to make waves. They are often timid and shy, wanting to blend in and not be noticed.

7. Overly Buttoned Clothes

People who are immaculately dressed and well-groomed with a sharp, buttoned-down look may be highly disciplined and well-organized. They may also be rigid and inflexible. These are the kind who press their blue jeans and iron their underwear; they cannot function unless everything is neat and orderly.

8. Inappropriate Clothes

Those who are inappropriately dressed for an occasion tell us they are nonconformists, rebels, and need to be noticed. People who wear sneakers to a black-tie affair, show up in jeans when the dress calls for cocktail attire, or women who dress sexily at work are guilty of this behavior.

   People who dress inappropriately may be showing signs of belligerence and inner hostility, as well as a desire to control situations. When they exhibit this behavior through inappropriate clothing, they are demonstrating a bullyish mentality that bespeaks insecurity.

9. Tasteful Clothes

People who dress for the occasion in a tasteful, clean, and stylish manner show they are cooperative and open. They tend to respect others and the situation they are in. These people may also purposely add a unique article of dress—an accessory, a special outfit, or a particular quality of clothing—to reflect their unique personalities and make a fashion statement. They do this as a reflection of their healthy, positive sense of self-esteem. They may also do this to invite discussion of their clothing or accessories, so that they can engage others in conversation.

Grooming and Hygiene

The way people are groomed says a great deal about their personality.

Cleanliness

Slovenly people usually suffer from poor self-esteem. They may be depressed or not even care what others think. They are usually in their own world and have no clue that their breath may be foul enough to bowl someone over, or that they need to use deodorant. These people often have stuff in the corners of their eyes, food on their face, or spittle on their lips when they speak.

Conversely, cleanliness implies self-esteem.

Hair Grooming

Men who wear toupees or have their hair combed over to the side are insecure and not forthcoming. They tend to hide things and aren't open about themselves.

Similarly, women who constantly change their hairstyles and hair color are saying they aren't satisfied with themselves and are searching for an identity. They, too, suffer from insecurity and low self-esteem.

Men and women who wear their hair in unusual colors or outrageous styles—like shaving their head on one side and having hair flowing down the other side—are screaming to be noticed.

Nail Grooming

Women with super-long, impractical nails may be saying, "Notice me!" People with nails bitten to the quick are usually nervous, anxious, and insecure. This self-mutilation is a form of self-destructiveness. In essence, they are taking their inner hostility or anger out on themselves.

Overly Meticulous Grooming

Good grooming says people care about themselves. But if they are so meticulously groomed that every hair has to be in place at all times, it says they are rigid, inflexible, and insecure.

For example, women who keep reapplying makeup reflect an insecurity. I remember when I was a freshman in college, we had a fire drill one morning. A young lady who lived in the dorm actually refused to leave her room until she applied her makeup. She was too insecure and self-conscious to be seen without it and would rather die in a fire than be seen "bare-faced."

On the other hand, when a woman wears no makeup, it says they may not care about their looks or may be natural, earthy types who have a "what you see is what you get" attitude.

Now we're ready to discuss the last of the four codes, the facial code.

CHAPTER 8

Understanding the Facial Code

Reading a person's body or facial language may be a better barometer than the words he or she speaks. As Sigmund Freud said, "He who has eyes to see and ears to hear may convince himself that no mortal can keep a secret. If his lips are silent, he chatters with his fingertips. Betrayal oozes out of him at every pore."

Just as there is vocal leakage, there is facial leakage. A person may attempt to mask an emotion, but for a millisecond the true expression is revealed. As Freud observed, it is almost impossible to hide true feelings.

Faces have told us much throughout the centuries, from the works of Rembrandt and Velazquez to modern day photojournalists and videographers. Expressions we have seen in classic photographs are etched in our minds forever. Who can forget the emotion captured in the face of Lee Harvey Oswald when he was shot by Jack Ruby, or the fear and agony in the face of the young naked Vietnamese girl, Kim Phuc, as she ran screaming in agony after being caught in a rain of napalm during a Vietnamese air strike? Or the picture of joy and elation when gymnast Mary Lou Retton won her Olympic gold medal, then jumped into the arms of her elated and beaming coach, Bela Karolyi. Or President Clinton's humbled and saddened expression as he told the nation he had not been forthright and that he did, indeed, have improper relations with "that woman." There is no question that these facial images and many others like them show us what is going on inside people.

Facial Code Survey

Here are some things to look for when analyzing a person's facial code.

1. Does the person have a steady gaze and look at you often?
2. Does the person seldom look at you when they are around you?
3. Does the person mirror your smile or nod the head at the same time you do?
4. Do the pupils enlarge when the person looks at you?
5. Do the eyes crinkle up at the corners when the person smiles at you?
6. Do the eyes look sad or nonanimated, even though the corners of the lips are turned up into a smiling position?
7. Are the eyes opened widely, exposing the whites above the iris while the jaw is dropped?
8. Does the person have a wide-eyed appearance and are the lips drawn back in a horizontal position?
9. Are the lower eyelids tense and are the eyebrows curved into an arch?
10. Is there tense eye contact whereby the upper and lower lids are narrowed?
11. Does the person look at you for a long period of time with an unflickering gaze?

12. Does the person have a soft, natural gaze when looking at you?

13. Does the person maintain a steady gaze when speaking with you without breaking to glance away for a moment?

14. Does the person narrow the eyes and furrow the forehead while simultaneously lifting up one eyebrow, as if in doubt?

15. Does the person raise the eyes up toward the ceiling when speaking with you?

16. Does the person give you a side glance as opposed to looking at you directly?

17. Does the person look at you sideways and lower the head while speaking with you?

18. Does the person look downward and avoid eye contact when around you?

19. Is there a firm and fixed gaze with the eye muscles in a relaxed state?

20. Does the person have an eye twitch or tic?

21. Does the person blink the eyes excessively when speaking?

22. Does the person break the gaze first?

23. Does the person raise the eyebrows and widen the eyes when first greeting you?

24. Does the person knit the eyebrows?

25. Does the person lower the eyebrows, press the lips together, and flare the nostrils when speaking to you?

26. Does the person often yawn when speaking with you?

27. Does the person swallow hard or gulp after you mention something favorable about yourself?

28. Does the person show the teeth, raise the cheeks, and turn the corners of the lips up when smiling?

29. Does the person have a tight or phony-looking grin?

30. Does the person smile inappropriately?

31. Does the person cover the mouth with the hand when speaking?

32. Does the person bite the lower lip?

33. Does the person often lick the lips?

34. Is there a cheek crease whereby the corner of the mouth is drawn back so it looks like a distorted smile?
35. Are the cheeks flushed?
36. Do the cheeks appear to droop or sag?
37. Does the chin jut forward when the person speaks?
38. Is the chin retracted?
39. Does the person support the chin with the hand?
40. Does the person stroke the chin lightly?
41. Is the chin lifted, making it appear as though the person is looking down at you?
42. Does the person often rub the chin along with other parts of the face?
43. Does the person often touch the nose when speaking?
44. Does the person wrinkle up the nose when speaking with you?
45. Does the person turn the nose up when speaking with you?
46. Does the person scratch behind the ear?
47. Does the person tug or pull on the earlobes or ear?
48. Does the person rub the ear between thumb and forefinger?
49. Does the person have an aloof or deadpan expression?
50. Does the face look alive and animated when the person is speaking with you?
51. Does the person have a relaxed and pleasant facial expression when speaking with you?

The purpose of this survey is to make you acutely aware of what people are doing with their faces when they speak with you. Looking at the nuances of a person's expression and mannerisms gives you an entirely different view of their face, one that you have probably never seen before. This will help you become a better observer.

Most of us don't realize that we know the language of the face very well. We tend to take this information for granted. After all, a person's face is a billboard of emotional life, a place where no words are needed to communicate. No matter what the ethnic or cultural background, everyone shares the same facial expressions for various emotions and can recognize emotions regardless of their background. Studies have shown that even infants are clearly able to recognize facial expression, having developed these expressions themselves.

Throughout this chapter, I will discuss what various facial expressions mean and how people communicate emotions through facial language. This chapter will explain the significance of the facial gestures mentioned in the survey, to help you become adept at deciphering the facial code.

Facial Disconnects

Researchers have shown that 55 percent of nonverbal communication is facial. A person can have the right words and say everything your ears want to hear, and say it in a sensuous, elegant, resonant tone that makes your ears perk up. But if the facial expressions are incongruous with what is said, that person may have well said nothing.

Several years ago I was introduced to two couples at a cocktail party. I noticed all four people seemed to be gritting their teeth, clenching their jaws, and wearing the tightest of smiles. As the people spoke, they gazed at one another in a lackluster way, although the conversation was quite pleasant. I began to feel uncomfortable because I sensed there was tension between the couples. So I excused myself and proceeded to mingle.

Later that evening, I ran into one of the couples I'd met earlier. I noticed their entire demeanor had changed. Their faces were relaxed and their expressions seemed happier and much more alive. Their smiles seemed real and genuine. I no longer noticed clenching jaw movements.

"Where are your friends—the other couple you were with?" I innocently asked. I wasn't too surprised when I heard their response.

"Thank goodness they left," said the wife. "Those two think they know everything. They are such know-it-alls but you never know where someone might end up someday. We heard that Joe may get promoted and would run my husband, Jim's, division. So we had to be nice."

Their words confirmed what I had already observed. Jim and his wife were tension-filled people who weren't comfortable talking to Joe and his wife. The longer I stood next to them, the more I realized it.

Facial Attraction

The eyes are one of the most powerful areas of communication. They tell us whether we are the object of someone's attention or whether someone is hostile toward us.

How can you tell if someone really likes you? In the way a person looks at you. If a person likes you, they look at you more often. If someone really likes you, the person will look longer than the normal two- or three-second gaze. In addition, the pupils get larger. When the pupils enlarge, this signals a positive emotional reaction.

Someone who avoids eye contact is either painfully shy or has something to hide. The person may not be able to look at you because of trying to hide that he or she is attracted to you. Conversely, when that person has a steady gaze, chances are they are feeling calm and have a sense of security about themselves.

Other gazes also tell us if a person is attracted. The first sign is called the cross gaze, where the individual looks to the left, sweeps the eyes across your face, then gazes to the right, repeating this movement without settling the gaze on you.

Another signal is when the person's eyebrows barely rise. The facial muscles slacken, the lower jaw drops slightly, but the lips remain sealed so the bottom half of the face looks longer. This is the look of someone who likes you but is a bit disappointed because you may not be returning the interest.

We have all heard the expression "Imitation is the sincerest form of flattery." So, if you find someone is mirroring your smile or nodding the head at the same moment you are, or putting a hand under the chin after you have done the same thing, rest assured that this person admires or likes you.

The more of these behaviors people do in common, the more they like one another. The next time you observe a couple, pay close attention to how they mimic each other and how many things they do gesturally that are similar. If they return smiles and gesture in a similar manner, you may be witnessing a couple falling in love or already in love.

Knowing Feelings by Eye Reading

Ramona went to her first college mixer. She was nervous and shy as she glanced around the room for a friendly face. She saw Kevin, who immediately caught her eye and smiled. They met and began to chat. Throughout the conversation, Kevin continued to look at Ramona and smile. She liked that. She felt comfortable and secure with him. She felt good about their interaction.

Suddenly, Darryl, a good friend of Kevin's whom he hadn't seen for a while, came up to them and enthusiastically greeted Kevin. Darryl gave Ramona a cursory greeting and continued speaking to Kevin. Although Kevin tried to involve Ramona in their conversation, Darryl made no eye contact with Ramona.

Whenever she spoke, Darryl looked away. Finally Ramona got the message. Darryl didn't like her and didn't want her around his friend. The more we like a person, the more we look at them. Conversely, the more we dislike an individual, the less we look at them.

Lying Eyes

If a person is smiling at you, you know if they are being sincere by their eyes. In a study conducted by Tamara Newman at the National Center for Post-Traumatic Stress Disorders in Boston, sixty women who had previously been identified as being anxious or repressive were videotaped. Although they turned their lips up in an expression of happiness, they repressed their true feelings. These were reflected in their unhappy, unsmiling eyes.

If you look at a photo of someone smiling and cover their lips, their eyes will reveal everything about their feelings. The eyes may look extremely sad, even though the lips may be curved in an uplifted smile.

If their cheeks aren't lifted and the nose hasn't spread, the person may not be very happy. This is because a real smile lights up the whole face—especially the eyes. Where there is no wrinkling at the corners or no movement in the region of the forehead, it is a fake, deceptive smile. People may not be happy even though they say they are.

Emotional Eyes

Observing the nuances of facial expressions can be important in reading a person. We can tell if someone is happy, surprised, afraid, bored, or sympathetic just by the subtle movement of their eyes.

1. Eyes of Surprise

When a person is surprised or taken off guard, it clearly shows in their eyes. Someone who is astonished will open the eyes extremely wide and show the sclera (the white of the eye) above the iris (the colored portion of the eye). The eyebrows are raised and curved upward, while the lower jaw often drops, allowing the lips to part.

As you become aware of responses you may be able to catch someone by surprise, especially after confronting the person in a lie. If you see this facial expression, chances are you caught the person in the act.

2. Scared Eyes

A person who is afraid will also have a wide-eyed appearance. The eyes seem locked open as if to catch the slightest action that may indicate impending peril. The lower eyelids are tense and the eyebrows are raised, unlike the person who is surprised, a fearful person's eyebrows are drawn together while the lips are drawn back into a horizontal position.

3. Angry Eyes

A person who is angry will gaze directly at the person with whom he or she is angry. There is tense eye-to-eye contact with both the upper and lower eyelids tense and narrowed, making the eyes appear "scrunched up." When someone focuses on you with an unflickering gaze, he or she may be attempting to intimidate, dominate, or threaten you.

4. Staring Eyes

If we stare too intensely at another person, it means one of two things are going on. A stare can either be regarded as a sexual advance—either welcome or unwelcome—or it can be a hostile act. Whether you are a chimpanzee, gorilla, dog, or human, staring is no good. If this fixed glance is held in place without a change in facial expression for any length of time, the person being stared at feels increasingly uncomfortable.

I was recently invited to a boxing match in Las Vegas. It was my first live fight. I was awed by the way the fighters stared at one another in the ring just before the fight in an attempt to intimidate one another.

People who are Machievellian also tend to stare. These people usually have a controlled gaze, rather than one that is soft and natural. They are adept at lying, and they have learned to control their anxiety levels by staring at others in order to manipulate them.

5. Doubting Eyes

If, simultaneously, the eyes narrow, the forehead furrows, and one of the eyebrows lifts, the person probably doubts what you have said. This expression often occurs when someone is unsure about a decision.

6. Astonished Eyes

When someone is utterly surprised, the eyes are raised, staring at the ceiling. An expression of disdainful astonishment may happen when someone doesn't believe you or doesn't believe something is really happening. This expression occurs when someone cannot believe what he or she has just seen or heard.

7. Shy Eyes

When a person is shy or embarrassed, he or she will often give someone a sideways glance instead of maintaining direct eye contact.

This is also considered a flirtatious action, whereby the person looks sideways at the other person while lowering the head and looking downward, much like a child does when feeling embarrassed or self-conscious.

Anthropologist Desmond Morris says this action is a conflicting movement because it signals "bold shyness," which are contradictory terms. In essence, it is an absence of forthright staring, combined with the humility of demurely looking away. Depending upon the situation, doing this can be either appealing or irritating to others.

8. Sad Eyes, Shameful Eyes

A person who is sad, embarrassed, or ashamed tends to look downward to avoid eye contact. The brow may also be wrinkled. Usually when a person breaks the gaze, he or she is either sad or submissive.

9. "I Didn't Do It!" Eyes

Just as a person who is lying will avoid eye contact, when we tell the truth and are sure of ourselves, especially after we have been falsely accused, we make strong and direct eye contact. The muscles around our eyes will be relaxed and provide a firm and fixed gaze.

10. Twitching Eyes

When we do things we shouldn't, our body often finds a way to tell us something is wrong. I once had a client who was engaged to a man she had no business being engaged to. He was a heavy drinker and she was always searching for him in bars. Immediately after this woman got engaged, she developed an involuntary eye twitch. It did not go away until six months later, when she broke off her engagement. Another client had a daughter who developed an eye twitch after she went to work in her controlling and bullying father's law firm. As soon as she quit, the twitch went away.

An eye twitch is a muscle contraction, or spasm, usually brought about by tension and stress. So if you happen to develop one, think about what is going on in your life. It may be a warning that you are stressed out: take heed!

11. Excessively Blinking Eyes

Excessive eye blinking may be a form of nervousness or insecurity. I once had a news anchor client who blinked excessively on the air. Even though she was well spoken, deep down she was worried about her contract renewal. Her discomfort about the fact she ultimately might not have a job manifested in her eye blinking.

After long discussions about her business, including setting forth alternatives in the event she wasn't rehired, she began to relax. We decided that news anchoring wasn't her only option. Our sessions worked beautifully. The next time she appeared on air, the excessive blinking stopped completely. After she relaxed and stopped worrying about her future, her eyes relaxed and she ended up getting a three-year contract renewal.

Excessive eye blinking also occurs when a person doesn't tell the truth or is worried or insecure about not being believed.

12. Avoiding Eyes

There is definitely something wrong when a person doesn't look directly at you. A person may avoid eye contact because he or she doesn't like you, isn't interested in you, is unable to confront you, or is intimidated by you. In most instances, people who lie will do what they can to avoid eye contact. They are plagued with guilt, so they don't want to face you.

But just because someone looks away doesn't necessarily mean he or she is lying. The person may feel uncomfortable or defensive and may have something to hide. People may avoid a direct gaze because they don't want others to know who they really are. They may be suffering from low self-esteem, so they look away, hoping you won't find them out.

Eyebrow Expressions

If you want to know if a person likes you, watch the eyebrows. When someone meets you for the first time and smiles, their eyebrows will automatically "flash," which means they will rise rapidly, and then go back down. This facial action occurs only once and is always accompanied by a smile. We tend to open our eyes wider when we increase our attention toward someone. If the other person does the same thing, rest assured you are on the right track. That person is interested in you. If, on the other hand, there is no flash, it means they probably couldn't be bothered.

Knitted Brows, Raised Brows, Lowered Brows

When someone doesn't like you or is anxious, he or she will "knit" the brow: simultaneously raise the eyebrows and draw them toward each other. It is, according to Desmond Morris, a contradictory expression, whereby the muscles try both to raise and to lower the brows. It is an expression that contains elements of grief, pain, anger, and fear, which combine to form anxiety.

Raising of the brows occurs when someone is shocked or in disbelief. Lowering of the brows—with the eyebrows drawn together and vertical lines between them—signifies anger.

Read My Lips

The true intent of what someone is saying is found not necessarily in the words he or she speaks but in the way the mouth plays out the facial code. The lips, throat, and cheeks all give signals about a person's state of mind.

Genuine Smiles

A smile is one of the most powerful things we can give another person. In a genuine smile, the corners of the lips are turned up, the lips are parted with the teeth showing, the cheeks are raised, and there is a wrinkling around the corners of the eyes.

To test the power of a smile, give someone a heartfelt smile and watch what happens. If you aren't feeling particularly happy and don't feel like smiling, do it anyway. Just put your face in the genuine smiling position and employ some sense memory. Go back to an experience in your life when you were extremely happy and keep that thought. Now smile. You'll be amazed by the positive reactions.

Smiling is contagious. When you smile, others usually follow suit and any tension you may have felt toward another will be erased. You will discover that others will open up to you. You will meet more people because they will perceive you as being approachable.

Tight Grin

A tight grin is a phony grin. Remember when you were a kid and didn't want to be in that photo with your family? You weren't particularly happy being there, so you didn't act happy—you didn't smile. Then the photographer said, "Say cheese," and you repeated the word. When you finally got your photos back, your mouth looked like it was tight and smiling, but your eyes still looked unhappy.

What I have described here is a phony grin, the tight smile people force upon themselves. They really don't like you or they don't like to be in your presence, but they know in order to be civilized and social, they have to smile. And this is what results. Next time you see a person with dull eyes and a pulled-back "cheese" grin, realize that it's not genuine.

Tight-lipped smilers are not exhibiting their true feelings. In fact, anyone who exhibits this facial gesture while saying, "Don't worry about it," or "It's no big deal," is telling you just the opposite. There is indeed a problem and you have to worry—it does bother them.

Inappropriate Smiles

"Why are you smiling?" asked Linda. "I just told you I lost my father. What's wrong with you?" That's what Linda said to her best friend, Sherol, when she told her that her father had passed away. Sherol wasn't being cruel or insensitive, but was expressing her intense nervousness and discomfort at a sad situation. Unfortunately, she expressed it with a smile instead of a frown.

People who smile during tension-filled crisis situations often end up causing additional grief. They are not necessarily sadistic; they are showing their discomfort with the situation. But that doesn't help those like Linda, who are shocked and dismayed at the reaction.

This very reaction occurred with former president Jimmy Carter, who many believed lost a second term in office because of inappropriate facial communication skills. Whenever he appeared on television and spoke of the ongoing Iranian hostage crisis, he would smile nervously, which made people feel extremely uncomfortable. It detracted from his credibility and trustworthiness. "Why is this man smiling when such an awful event is occurring?" thought most Americans. What they didn't realize was that the former president was expressing his nervousness through his inappropriate smile. His serious and sad words did not match his happy and upbeat facial expression. It made him appear weak as a leader.

The next time you see someone smiling after they hear of an unfortunate event, understand that they usually can't help themselves. It is simply an automatic reaction to being nervous and uneasy.

Yawning

Usually we think nothing of someone yawning when we speak, other than the fact they may be bored or tired. But psychologists now believe there is a deeper meaning to yawning. It may be an escape mechanism used for not confronting difficult, painful, or stressful issues.

When people bring up something they don't want to deal with, they often subconsciously yawn in order to avoid the subject.

I had a client whose son was a terror in school. He always cut class and was on his way to becoming a juvenile delinquent. When my client spoke of her son and we discussed her role as a parent, she would inevitably let out a yawn. It was uncanny to watch. She couldn't deal with the fact she was too permissive and an absentee parent.

Gulping

"Oh, I'm really happy for you," said Jessica, gulping. "It's so great that you are going to have a baby! It's exciting," she said, gulping again. A monotonous tone, and the hard swallow or "gulp" (where you see the Adam's apple move up and down) is an obvious give-away about how someone feels about you or a situation.

Rather than being happy that her friend was going to have a baby, Jessica was actually quite jealous. She was in shock, so her autonomic nervous system took over. Her mouth got dry and she had to swallow hard to stop from choking with jealousy. What she really wanted to say was, "I can't stand you. I am terribly jealous of you. You get everything you want in life and now you are going to have a baby. Look at me, sitting babyless and husbandless."

The next time you meet someone new or you tell someone something great that's happened to you, watch the neck. It will reveal how the person really feels about the things you've said. A hard swallow accompanied by a tight grin, dead eyes, and a lifeless voice, is a dead giveaway that this person is *not* pleased to see you, no matter what words he or she actually uttered.

Hand to Mouth

Often when a child tells a lie, he or she will cover the mouth in an attempt to subconsciously retract the lie that has just come out. As we become older, these become natural reactions. Covering the mouth may be a sign of deception. Like the child, they are saying, "I shouldn't have said that," as they cover their mouth.

When an adult puts a hand to the mouth while speaking or touches the lips, he or she is probably not telling the truth. If you want to determine whether someone likes what you are saying, see if they bring their forefinger to their lips. They are subconsciously and silently "shushing" you.

A client of mine who was a very controversial public speaker noticed audience members kept bringing their hands to their mouths as he spoke. He told them, "I know many of you find what I have just reported to be incredible and difficult to understand, but if you take the time to listen carefully and digest what I have said, you will find there is a lot of merit in what I have to tell you."

As soon as he made this remark, the people in the audience immediately changed their body and facial positions, assuming a more attentive posture, and most were no longer covering their mouths. They weren't subliminally "shushing" him and were more receptive to hearing what he had to say. He took his cue from watching their facial code.

Lip Biting

Biting or gnawing the lips is often a controlled expression of internalized anger or resentment. This is basically a safe way to express hostility. Biting the lower lip while shaking the head is a display of intense anger.

The late Princess Diana used to bite her lip a lot, as evidenced in numerous photographs. She may have done this in an attempt to suppress hostile feelings toward the intrusions of photographers.

Lip Licking

People lick their lips for a variety of reasons. It may indicate that an individual is not telling the truth or is expressing nervousness. Often when people are nervous the mouth will get dry, so they will automatically lick their lips as a means to create saliva. People who drink or smoke a lot often have dry lips and tend to lick them a lot.

Lip licking may also be seen as a flirtatious habit. Depending on how seductively it is done, it may be intended to attract the attention of others in a sexual way.

Cheeky Talk

A person's cheeks also have a language of their own. Cheek movement can tell you if someone is genuinely happy or is being sarcastic. When a person exhibits a genuine smile, their cheeks will be raised. By contrast, someone who presents a tight-lipped grin or phony smile will have cheeks that are flat and drooped.

When you want to know if someone is being sarcastic or has hostile or doubtful feelings toward you, observe the cheek. For example, when one corner of the mouth is drawn back strongly so it forms a crease in the cheek (like a distorted smile), it means the person has inner resentment and a sarcastic comment or tone is sure to follow. Rubbing the cheek is an unconscious gesture indicating that a person doubts what you are saying.

Finally, cheeks will reveal if a person is embarrassed or even humiliated. Not only will the cheeks turn red, but they may appear to droop or sag, depending on the degree of humiliation the person is feeling.

The Emotional Chin

Anthropologist Desmond Morris believes we can tell a great deal about how to read others by observing lower face movements—the movements of the chin and jaw—especially in terms of determining emotional state.

1. Chin Anger

Someone who is angry tends to jut the chin forward, which commonly registers as a threatening or hostile act. You notice chin-jutting in small children who don't want to do what they are told. The first thing they do before they say no is jut their chin forward as a defiant gesture. Most of us carry this gesture into adulthood. We unconsciously jut our chins forward when we have been wronged or are about to tell someone off. During a conversation, you can tell if someone is getting angry by observing the position of the chin.

2. Chin Fear

When someone's chin is retracted, that person is exhibiting fear. A retracted chin is a protective reaction, much like a turtle does when it retreats into its shell. When we watch horror films, we tend to recoil, appearing to rest the chin on the neck. So when you see someone pull away by retracting the chin, he or she may be afraid of you or threatened by you.

3. Chin Boredom

When the chin is supported by the hand, it means the person is trying to focus attention, perhaps on whomever is speaking. Although the person may look thoughtful, the message is that he or she is bored and is holding up the head in order to concentrate better.

4. Chin Concentration

When someone strokes the chin lightly and gently, much like stroking a beard, it implies the person is concentrating heavily on what the speaker has said.

5. Chin Criticism and Snobbery

When someone is being highly critical or judgmental, they tend to lift the chin, sending the message "I am better than you," or "You don't know what you are talking about."

6. Chin Doubt

When someone distrusts what you are saying, the person often rubs or holds the chin, subconsciously holding back from telling you he or she doesn't believe you.

The Nose Knows

Touching the nose may be a subconscious act that says the person has something to hide, a sign that someone is being deceptive and not telling the truth. It may have to do with the involuntary move to cover the mouth for saying something he or she shouldn't, but instead, the person reaches for the nose.

Ruthie hadn't seen Todd, a college friend, in ages. She had put on a lot of weight through the years, which left her looking much older and less attractive. Throughout their conversation, it was apparent Todd didn't mean any of the compliments he directed toward her. As soon as he said, "You look great," his hand moved toward his nose. When he told her he liked her outfit, that she looked fabulous, or that he was glad to see her, he would unconsciously grab at his nose. Luckily his conversation with Ruthie didn't last too long or he would have rubbed his nose raw.

Sometimes when someone is speaking to you, you'll notice the person has wrinkled the nose, which usually means someone either disapproves or is disgusted by you.

We have all heard the expression about having one's "nose in the air." When the nose is raised and directed upward, with the head tilted back, it is a subconscious sign of snobbery, superiority, an "I am better than you" attitude. The person is being judgmental, reflected by turning up the nose. This gesture—the opposite of the shy person's lowering the head—may also reflect feelings of contempt, defiance, or dominance.

Ear Talk

Unconscious touching can also involve the ears. If someone scratches behind the ear with a bent forefinger, it means the person is confused and doubts what he or she is hearing, or may have misunderstood what was said.

When someone tugs at the ears while speaking, the person may be using a delay technique. He or she may have previously heard something and wants to think it over before responding.

Subconscious rubbing of the ears between the thumb and the forefinger says, "I really don't want to hear this." This gesture often appears when a person is not telling the truth and the other person knows it. It is a subconscious attempt to block the ears from hearing what is said. If you see someone doing this while you or someone else is speaking, that person is not interested in hearing what is being said, or simply doesn't believe it.

Aloof Expressions

An aloof or deadpan expression is an attempt to hide anger, resentment, or hostility. Everyone's face routinely exhibits some degree of muscle tension and animation, so when the face presents dead eyes and flaccid muscles, it signals that the person has given up and is resigned to the situation at hand.

Prison inmates resort to this type of facial nongesturing in order to show they are in control of their emotions. By appearing expressionless, they find they are less offensive and invasive toward others. They are less likely to enter someone's space and become a victim.

People who don't want you to know how angry or upset they are (passive-aggression) often show no expression. They don't want to give you power by letting you know you've upset them.

The Sincere Face

When someone is sincere and likes you, that person will look directly at you with a face that looks alive and exhibits a great deal of facial animation. The eyes do not wander. The gaze is not hard and steady, but soft and welcoming. The mouth is relaxed and the jaw is slightly dropped in a relaxed "rest position." The back teeth do not touch. There is usually a warm, sincere smile, where the corners of the lips turn up and the eyes are bright and wrinkled at the corners.

This type of facial expression says someone is confident, secure, open, and outwardly directed, as opposed to being uptight and closed in communication.

Now that you've learned the four codes of communication, you're ready to apply what you've learned. In Part Three, we'll move on to the fourteen personality profiles.

Using the Codes to Determine Personality Types

CHAPTER 9

Understanding the 14 Personality Profiles

Categorizing People

For centuries, much has been written about the classification of personality traits. The list is impressive, from the ancient Greek physician Galen, to Sigmund Freud and Carl Jung, to contemporary psychologists such as Abraham Maslow, Eric Erikson, Isabel Briggs Meyers, and David Keirsey.

Others, such as Kathleen Hurley, Theodore Dobson, Rene Baron, Elizabeth Wagle, and Don Risso, have incorporated the *enneagram,* a nine-pointed drawing, to illustrate a person's personality type. These nine types are helper, achiever, observer, romantic, confronter, peacemaker, succeeder, adventurer, and individualist.

Throughout the ages, we have had an insatiable need to unlock the mysteries of who we are, how we fit into the universe, and how we fare as compared to those around us. People have discovered that only through better understanding of themselves and others can they understand the miracle of the world around them.

Just as there are toxic people, there are also terrific and honorable people. When you understand the codes of communication, you can determine into which category they fall. A cute, upturned nose or a big, masculine jaw or straight teeth do not guarantee positive personality traits. Similarly, large ears and a huge, crooked nose don't denote bad personality traits.

In order to assess personality, we must look deeper than physical appearance. We must examine behavior—who they are, how they move, how they comport themselves, how they sound, and what they say.

Personality Profile Quiz

Take the following quiz to determine a person's primary personality profile. Go through the fourteen categories and answer the various questions in each category. If the majority of answers are yes, then the person's personality type would most likely fall into that specific category. You do not have to answer yes to *all* of the questions in a category for it to define a primary personality type. However, try to choose which characteristics appear to be the most dominant. Keep in mind that people may fall into several different personality categories.

1. Does the person keep things inside emotionally and then let it all out in a torrent of rage after it has been stored for a long time? Is it difficult for the person to give a straight answer? Does he or she say one thing verbally when the body language and facial expression are telling you something different?
2. Is the person overly complimentary? Does he or she use double entendres, or speak in a sensuous tone? Does the person rarely break eye contact? Does he or she touch others a lot?
3. Does the person often complain and constantly seem to be in the midst of one crisis after another? Does he or she tend to

speak in a whiney tone? Does the person appear to have a stoop-shouldered posture?

4. Does the person rarely let on how he or she feels emotionally? Is this a person of few words who rarely shares much about the self? Is the posture stiff and uptight? Is the voice a monotone? Is facial expression often lacking?

5. Does the person usually not have a point of view and seem to agree with what the majority of others are thinking? Does he or she not want to make waves? Is the voice often soft, with hesitant, mumbling tones? Does the person appear uncomfortable when forced to give an opinion, as shown by facial expression and body movement?

6. Does the person tend to go off on tangents? Does he or she tell you more than you need to know? Does he or she often speak hesitantly? Does he or she go to either extreme of making very poor eye contact or staring at you without breaking eye contact? Does he or she often shrug the shoulders when speaking? Do the facial and body expressions show discomfort?

7. Does the person constantly talk about himself or herself, showing little interest in any other topic? Does he or she constantly seek praise? Does he or she speak loudly, becoming the center of attention when talking?

8. Does the person consistently make derogatory remarks about others in order to seem superior? Does he or she speak in a condescending manner, like a know-it-all? Is the posture rigid? Does the facial expression indicate that the person appears literally to be looking down upon or judging others?

9. Does the person usually seem to be interrupting others or trying to top whatever anyone else says? Does he or she show off, purporting to be better and have more than others? Do the voice, facial expression, and body language appear tense and rigid?

10. Does the person express himself or herself openly? Does he or she use a great deal of emotion to readily express true

feelings? Is there sincerity in what the person says? Is he or she a good listener? Is his or her touch firm and direct?

11. Does the person use loud, attacking, brash tones? Does he or she consistently make sarcastic negative remarks or cutting comments? Is the person stubborn, acting like they know-it-all? Does he or she make a lot of noise and commotion when moving around? Is there often a tense or angry expression on the face?

12. Is this person the life of the party? Is he or she quick with comebacks or witty remarks? Does the person always seem to need to be the center of attention? Does he or she speak in a bouncy exuberant tone? Is he or she usually in perpetual motion? Are the body movements highly animated?

13. Does the person often make faux pas after faux pas? Does he or she seem to speak before thinking, saying whatever comes to mind? Is the person preoccupied with his or her own thoughts? Is he or she extremely blunt and overly direct? Does he or she tend to flit from topic to topic? Is the person oblivious to social convention—how close he or she sits or stands next to others or whether gestures are expansive?

14. Is the person sensitive to others? Is he or she verbally generous, speaking politely and seeming genuinely interested in what others have to say? Does he or she usually speak positively about others? Does the person say what he or she means and mean what he or she says? Is there a robustness and enthusiasm to the speech? Is there usually a pleasant and open facial expression? Is the person receptive to others? Does he or she appear to be physically relaxed and comfortable around others?

What Your Answers Mean

Look at all of your yes answers for each of the fourteen categories. Determine which category has more yes answers. Match the number of the category above with the number of the personality type listed below and you will then discover the person's personality profile.

When you analyze someone's personality, it is essential that you look at them objectively, then go a step deeper by looking at them emotionally. Before you read a person to determine personality type, remember that the most important consideration in reading people is consistency. Remember that human beings are not inanimate objects. People can and do change, so they need to be observed over time before you can certify results. Perhaps they behaved a certain way years ago, even months ago, then a life-changing circumstance occurred and altered the way they view life. Hence their personality traits may change temporarily or permanently.

1. The Passive aggressor
2. The Seducer
3. The Victim
4. The Icicle
5. The Wimp
6. The Liar
7. The Narcissist
8. The Snob
9. The Competitor
10. The Giver
11. The Bully
12. The Jokester
13. The Unconscious one
14. The Real dealer

As you read through this chapter, you will find a detailed analysis of each of the personality profiles. You will learn in greater detail what to look for in a person's speech, voice, facial, and body language to assist you further in determining what type of personality profile a person possesses.

Psychological Considerations

In analyzing personality types, you will usually be examining people who are relatively intact psychologically. These people may be suffering from certain neuroses (as most of us do) but are still able to function adequately.

It is important to know there are those who are not able to function due to more serious psychological problems, such as schizophrenia, whereby a person may be out of touch with reality and may exhibit bizarre speaking patterns that may not make sense to others. Or someone may exhibit specific facial and body movements that indicate they are out of control.

Similarly, some may suffer from bipolar disorder, or may have severe bouts with depression. There may be distinct vocal and speech patterns ranging from pressured speech to hyperloquaciousness to communicating about grand illusions to minimal monotone speech to lack of speaking at all. Facial and body movements may be consistent with their disorders, from hyperactivity to barely moving facial and body muscles.

Those with borderline personality disorders may also have difficulty socializing with others. That may be reflected by what and how they say things and the serious, often angry looks that appear on their faces.

Addressing these psychological problems is beyond the scope of this book. Suffice it to say, we must be sensitive to the fact these conditions do exist, and must keep this fact in mind when attempting to analyze personality traits.

First Impressions

Most of the time you only have one chance to see and hear a person in order to form an impression. You may have one opportunity to decide whom to work with or employ or befriend. That is why it is essential to comprehensively observe people. The more you practice looking for certain vocal, speaking, facial, and body language patterns, the easier it will become for you to read another person accurately.

It doesn't take much time to form an opinion about someone. That impression can come in a matter of seconds. The daunting thing about first impressions is they may be based on little information. For instance, someone may not like you because you resemble someone who refused to date that person in high school. Or you may remind someone of a relative he or she can't stand, or you may be wearing a style of clothing the person doesn't like. You may belong to an ethnic group someone has had a bad experience with. In all these cases, you're liable to be unfairly categorized.

Unfortunately, people who judge others in this manner make their decisions based upon prejudice, intolerance, and ignorance. This chapter is designed to help you stop making such snap decisions. It will provide you with information and data about specific personality types, so you will form opinions based on accuracy and wisdom.

In this day and age, where there is so much confusion about others, information can shed light upon your life and change it for the better.

The Fourteen Personality Types

After years of reviewing literature in the field of communication, acquiring data and doing empirical research in my private practices in Beverly Hills and New York City, and conducting research while serving as a university professor, I have discovered there are ways in which people with specific personality types tend to speak and comport themselves.

You may have similar observations without even realizing it. Think back to your high school days, when you may have had a dispute with someone. Now think back to each decade of your life that has followed. Try to recall the people with whom you've had dispute. Remember the way they spoke to you and what they said. How did they look at you, and how did they carry themselves during the course of your relationship? Now try to recall those with whom you've gotten along famously. Think about their speaking patterns, facial expressions, and body language.

You will begin to see patterns emerge. You will be able to categorize people according to their personality type, based upon the way they communicated with you. You will see that the bullying people had loud, choppy, staccato voices, and always seemed to have a scowl on their face. Remember the furrowed brows, broad movements, and pointed accusatory fingers—it was all about intimidation.

You'll realize those effervescent, resonant speakers always meant what they said and said what they meant. They never failed to greet you with a smile and looked you right in the eye when they spoke. They animatedly used their hands and arms to express the importance of what they were saying and they leaned into you when they spoke. You got the impression they were genuinely interested and truly appreciated you. They were the real deal as far as you were concerned. They were honest, sincere people who really cared.

You will notice there are more toxic categories than terrific ones, for two reasons. First, I have included more toxic types to give you greater insight into recognizing those who may be harmful so that you can protect yourself. Second, I have included the majority of positive personality traits in the real deal category because many of the traits that these people possess are the opposite of the toxic traits.

I will expand upon these toxic and terrific people by describing them in terms of the four codes of communication—speech, vocal, body language, and facial codes. By integrating all four communication codes, you will be able to create a seamless impression about someone's personality. Although you can often detect important clues by using one communication code, the most accurate judgment comes when using all four codes simultaneously, so you may detect someone's essential truth—the core of who that person really is.

1. The Passive Aggressor

Speech Code

Passive aggressors may say they are "really happy" for you and use all the right words, but in truth they are not happy for you at all. Their monotone delivery belies their words.

They will cast a sarcastic comment, or they will throw something at you that you may have shared in confidence. This may be followed by their ever-popular "I was only kidding" expression. They may also fawn over you and sing your praises, even when you don't deserve it.

Some passive aggressors don't speak a lot but say what is on their mind. They may suddenly let you have it as they let fly with verbal venom they've stored for years. They usually withhold their true feelings and will only let them out after they have exploded.

They are also the kind who won't give a straight answer. They tend to limit what they say and don't reveal much information. They tend to say, "I don't know," when you ask their opinion about something.

Vocal Code

Passive aggressors start off their communication strong and upbeat, then tend to trail off, making it difficult for them to be understood. They also have a tendency to speak softly, so they can barely be heard. They get others to pay attention by making them ask them to speak up. This is nothing more than a control mechanism.

They may use a higher-pitched voice that is overly bouncy and sickeningly sweet in tone. Someone who employs this vocal technique may be overcompensating for miserable feelings harbored toward you or others.

Another way they harbor inner anger is by not opening their jaws when they speak, sounding nasal like the lockjaw nasalers. Other passive aggressors may harbor anger and jealousy toward you, which can be heard in their monotone. Finally, passive aggressors may laugh and cough to suppress how they really feel.

Body Language Code

Passive aggressors may touch a lot in their attempt to overcompensate against their ill feelings. They may fidget a great deal or rock back and forth in a subconscious attempt to get out. Despite verbal pleasantries, they really don't like you.

You may witness foot tapping, finger drumming, and other extraneous hand and foot gestures, indicating they want to leave. In addition, even though the body may be facing you when they are speaking to you, their toes may be pointed in the opposite direction, hinting that they don't want to be with you.

Their hands may be in a fist with the thumbs hidden, which indicates hostile feelings. You may also see their ankles in a locked position when they are seated, indicating they are withholding information. Their head may jerk when they speak or they may rub their neck, indicating they are repressing thoughts.

They may also lean toward you—a sign they are interested in what you have to say—followed by immediately leaning back, which indicates ambivalent feelings. They may exhibit a bone-crushing handshake, which further indicates ill feelings. When speaking to you, they may not use their hands, or they may hold on to themselves as a means of getting a grip on their negative feelings.

Facial Code

Passive aggressors often have a tight-lipped, phony grin. Their lips are not turned up at the corners, nor do they show other manifestations of a true smile. They may also bite their lower lip in a subconscious attempt to control feelings of anger.

2. The Seducer

Speech Code

Expert verbal seducers are brimming with charm in order to get what they want. They use seductive ways to wield power. Seducers often make sexual comments or use double entendres and have little compunction about exaggerating or stretching the truth if it makes another person feel good. They are extraordinarily complimentary, saying whatever the other person needs to hear. They constantly flirt and tend to crave attention because it fuels their ego.

Initially, seducers' topics of conversation are focused on others' needs, concerns, and interests. When seducers become more familiar with their verbal prey, the topic of conversation shifts to them—their own needs, concerns, and interests. They are especially fond of using the "poor me" tactic—sharing their woes to gain sympathy and attention. They will fawn over another person and stop at nothing to say something pleasing so they will be liked.

They do all this to manipulate others, because they are extremely insecure and have a great need to be loved. They tend to manipulate those who show them love in order to establish power over them. Their constant requests lead to physical conquests, which fuel their fragile egos.

They have little remorse when they have lied to another person. If the person finds out and confronts them, they often verbally wiggle out of the situation. They will do whatever it takes and say whatever they must to get their way. Once seducers have gotten what they want from someone, they are on to their next verbal conquest.

Vocal Code

Female seducers often have a cutesy, high-pitched, breathy tone. They may also exhibit a lisp and a tendency to giggle. Male seducers sound breathy and use a lower than normal pitch in order to sound sexy and vocally appealing. Both sexes speak in soft, mellifluous tones and laugh a lot.

Body Language Code

Seducers usually tilt their head in the direction of the person to whom they are speaking in an attempt to show they are truly interested. They nod in agreement whether they agree or not. Their aim is to get the other person to like them, to encourage interest. The head may be bowed with eyes gazing upward.

They usually mirror the behavior of those they are speaking to and it is not unusual to see seducers invade others' space. They get physically close in order to let others know they find them attractive. They use subtle touch to get their point across and to secure approval, "accidentally" brushing against someone, and the touch tends to linger, further demonstrating interest. They tend to lean their body into the person and remain close for a long period of time as a means of controlling the other.

Seducers often have a relaxed stance and are comfortable within their bodies. There is more forward tilting of shoulders and pelvis, and they will often roll their shoulders back, exposing their torsos in an attempt to get attention. They may move a leg in a slow, rhythmic pattern.

Seducers tend to play with their jewelry or their hair. They may also place their fingers on the neck or lips to draw attention to these body parts. They may be provocative or sexy dressers, another signal to prospective conquests.

Facial Code

Seducers never lose eye contact. They hold a gaze well beyond the usual two or three seconds. They are rarely seen without a smile on their faces or a twinkle in their eyes.

They tend to exhibit a number of seductive facial movements, such as a half smile, a slight lip pout combined with a fixed gaze. They often lick their lips. Often, pouty lower lip postures are used in a provocative manner.

3. The Victim

Speech Code

Victims tend to be chronic complainers. Their conversation seems to revolve around people in conflict. They are quick to blame others because they never see themselves at fault. Even when they are clearly wrong they will always find someone else to blame. It is not uncommon for them to put themselves down. They see themselves as life's sacrificial lambs.

Vocal Code

Victims often have weaker, higher-pitched voices that inflect upward at the end of sentences. It may sound muffled from time to time because they often tend to mumble and may exhibit a nasal whine. There is usually a softer tone that says, "Please don't attack me, I'm timid."

Their soft, monotonous tones reflect an internal sadness whereby they feel powerless and out of control. The boring tones make it difficult to communicate with them; they can't seem to get their message across.

Body Language Code

Victims are tentative in body language and posture. They slouch their shoulders, indicating their depressed state. They often fold their arms as a means of protection. The head is usually bowed and they tend to look up at people.

They frequently fidget when discussing points of view that make them accountable for their actions. In those cases, they tend to be restless and may rock back and forth when they speak.

It is not uncommon to see them wringing their hands or biting and picking their nails. They are unsure about themselves and extremely insecure. They tend to hold on to their arms or legs when they speak in order to feel more secure. They may sit with one leg tightly wrapped around the other in order to help ease their discomfort.

Facial Code

Victims' eyes seem to narrow when they speak due to muscle tension around the eyelids and eyebrows. The forehead is usually furrowed. They tend to look away when they speak. They do not maintain eye contact, indicating a difficulty in speaking. It is not uncommon for them to bite their lip as a sign of sadness and discomfort.

4. The Icicle

Speech Code

Icicles are not verbally generous and usually keep things to themselves, especially their feelings. When they do speak they may overly articulate words. You never know where they are coming from emotionally because they never let you know how they feel. They tend to be people of few words who only speak when spoken to and rarely initiate a conversation. Since their feelings rarely show, it is difficult to know what they are thinking.

They usually do what they are told and are extremely task-oriented. They may seem easygoing until, like the passive aggressor, they erupt in verbal violence when threatened.

Vocal Code

Icicles usually speak in a monotone, displaying little emotion when they talk. They are difficult to read because they rarely display emotion and tend to go by the book.

Body Language Code

Icicles usually have a ramrod-stiff posture. Their mechanical gestures often make others feel uneasy because they appear cold and inflexible.

They are guarded in their movements and usually don't touch. If they hug, it is often stiff and awkward. You often see them covering their body with their arms or crossing their arms over their chest. The head may be erect, further indicating their defensiveness and rigidity.

Icicles may seem to be judging others since they often keep their hands on their lap or steeple their fingers. Actually, this is their way of masking their own insecurities. They often have a weak handshake, reflecting an unwillingness to connect. They gesture with their thumb appearing straight up and fingers straight, which demonstrates their rigid positions.

They keep their distance since they dislike bonding. They also feel uncomfortable in situations outside their own regimen and organization.

Facial Code

Icicles often have a blank facial expression with a rigid jaw. The chin is often retracted, indicating they are on the lookout for physical or emotional threats. They don't make eye contact.

They may have a tight smile that reeks of insincerity. They often yawn when discussing something that makes them uncomfortable. You may also see them gulp when they talk about anything that deals with emotions.

5. The Wimp

Speech Code

Typically, wimps are people of few words. They often fail to say what is on their mind since they are afraid of making waves and upsetting the status quo. They tend to be timid. "I don't know" is a typical expression. They are usually afraid to commit themselves to a point of view. They are self-effacing and make negative comments about themselves. They always seem to put themselves down. Their vocabulary is reflective of their hopeless state; they speak in tentative terms and couch everything they say.

Vocal Code

Wimps exhibit a soft, monotonous voice. Their shaky vocal quality is often filled with hesitation and repetition. They may speak slowly to avoid mistakes or too rapidly in an attempt to get everything out.

Body Language Code

Wimps often scratch their heads to indicate confusion. They may offer a limp handshake to go with their uninspired vocal tone. They usually have a slouched posture with the shoulders rolled forward, indicating timidity. They may often rock back and forth as a display of their discomfort. Usually they fold their arms across their bodies as a means of protecting themselves. They may hold on to themselves or to an object to brace themselves when they experience tension and discomfort.

Facial Code

Wimps go to great lengths to avoid eye contact and are usually the first to break off a gaze if their eyes happen to meet another's.

They tend to have a frightened look on their faces and their eyes radiate fear and tension. Their eyebrows are often drawn together, further indicating fear. They bite the lower lip and tend to retract the chin, indicating lack of confidence. When they are forced to confront issues, their cheeks may turn red.

6. The Liar

Speech Code

Liars often go off on tangents and may tell you more than you need to know. They may also be evasive. They are circumlocutors, with words spoken in a roundabout fashion. Their speech is frequently peppered with "um," "er," "uh," and similar hesitations.

Like seducers, liars are brimming with charm in order to get what they want. They may also be two-faced and will often build you up then ultimately deflate you. If they bring information, they will usually pass information about you to others because it makes them feel important.

Vocal Code

Liars have a relaxed, lifeless tone. It is methodical as they ponder what they are going to say. But they may also sound bouncy and bubbly. The voice may be pitched higher when they are not being forthright.

Body Language Code

Male liars may loosen their ties while women liars may simply place their hands on their necks if they haven't told the truth. This is a sign of being "found out." They may also hide their hands as they speak, or fidget, rocking back and forth as they express their discomfort and uneasiness. Sometimes they do the opposite, sitting or standing perfectly still—too still, so they appear rigid.

People who lie may also not use hand gestures, since they have to think about the story they invented as opposed to telling the truth. So it is not uncommon to see their gestures decrease as they continue to speak.

Their feet may belie them. They may jiggle their feet rapidly up and down in the air to indicate their impatience. Their toes may also be positioned in the opposite direction of their torso, and pointed away from the person to whom they are lying. They also tend to shrug one of their shoulders when they make a disclaimer. Liars may touch others a lot, but it is hostile touching as a means of showing control.

Facial Code

Liars may do one of two things with their eyes. They will purposely not look at you when they speak, or they will stare right at you, rarely breaking eye contact. Their smiles are often forced and tight-lipped, with no crinkling around the eyes and with the lips merely pulled back. They may engage in other fake expressions as well.

There may be excessive eye-blinking, indicating they are insecure about something or that they may have something to hide or are just plain nervous. You may see them with their fingers over their lips or their hand over their mouths as they speak or listen.

7. The Narcissist

Speech Code

Narcissists talk about themselves constantly and have an insatiable need for praise. They may tell all about themselves, things you really don't want to hear. They will usually discuss inappropriate subjects as a means of shocking others into paying attention to them.

The words "I" and "my" are the most predominant words in their vocabulary. If the topic is not about them, they are not interested. To relieve their boredom, they inevitably turn the conversation toward themselves.

Vocal Code

Narcissists are often loud and may sound obnoxious. They intend to be heard by as many people as possible. They tend to have highly animated, upbeat voices when the topic is centered around them. Otherwise they usually exhibit a duller, more subdued tonal quality. They may even use a monotone, which indicates they are completely bored with the discussion.

Body Language Code

The stiff position narcissists may assume is done to make them look cool and important. They may lean back, slump over, or support their head with their hand when they speak about anything but themselves.

When they sit, their legs are often stretched in front of them, indicating an entitlement to take up room. They tend to use a great deal of arm and hand gestures to make their presence known. They also tend to touch freely to get others to focus attention on them.

Facial Code

Their smiles are forced if they are ignored. Otherwise they are bright and genuine, especially if others are paying attention. They seem to thrive and "light up" when acknowledged. When they are not looking in a mirror, they will give the person who is paying attention to them excellent eye contact, but they give this only when speaking and listening about themselves. If the topic centers around someone else, they will break eye contact as a means of displaying their lack of interest.

Their eyes dart around the room a lot as they are constantly on the lookout for important people and those who will pay the most attention to them. They usually look at others to see if they are looking at them.

8. The Snob

Speech Code

With their "I'm better than you" attitude, snobs are usually making some derogatory statement, which makes them feel a cut above others. Due to their profound insecurity, they need to cut others down to make themselves feel superior.

Like bullies, snobs have a tendency to put others down, although they do it in a more subtle fashion. Also like bullies, snobs display a mechanical rigidity to their speech as they attempt to control the conversation.

Snobs are often quick-tongued and always have an answer. They have a keen eye and are usually up on current topics. They thrive on gossip, especially the kind that makes the person being gossiped about look bad. This makes snobs feel elevated. They are fully aware of making the right connections in order to get ahead, so it is not uncommon to hear them fawning over others who may be socially significant.

The real reason for this snobbery is that it masks a deep insecurity. They talk in a condescending manner, showing off their knowledge as they pontificate for hours. They love to use trendy expressions or fancy words or phrases to show off and will tend to use ethnic flavoring in their speech or slang, with the intention of gaining power by making you uncertain about what they are saying.

Their biggest fear is being ostracized and left alone. They would rather speak to someone they deem socially inferior than wind up by themselves. Solitude appears to overwhelm them. Like narcissists, snobs need an audience. Also like the narcissist, snobs usually demonstrate an "I" quality to their speaking, centering around them and how much better they think they are. They seem to take forever telling a story and will usually ignore you if you try to interject. Like bullies and narcissists, snobs finish what they are going to say on their terms, not on yours.

Vocal Code

Snobs often have lockjaw when they speak, giving a tight, nasal quality to their voice. They usually speak in deliberate, choppy, well-articulated, staccato tones devoid of vocal animation, giving the tonal quality of someone who is highly critical. In addition, their hard glottal attacks indicate impatience at those they deem to be subordinate.

Body Language Code

Snobs often have a stiff, erect, rigid posture whereby they lean backward in an attempt to maintain an air of social distance between themselves and others. You may see them with arms akimbo, placed on their hips with elbows extended, a sign for others to keep their distance.

Usually they expose the back of their hands when they speak as an indication they are closed off to others. Their fingers may also be interlocked with thumbs rotating or fidgeting in a twiddling motion, indicating boredom.

Facial Code

The snob smile may be phony and forced, with the mouth drawn back so you can see the crease in the cheek. This sarcastic smile is filled with doubt while lacking respect.

When their pretentious side appears, snobs literally lift their chins and look down their nose. They may even close their lids with the eyebrows raised and lips pursed as they speak. This is an attempt to verbally cut off others. They will often jerk the heads backward when they don't like what another is saying.

Their eyes dart around the room as they hurriedly seek out people who are the most influential and can be of assistance to them.

9. The Competitor

Speech Code

Competitors interrupt a lot and try to top whatever you've said. If you say you have a cute dog, they will immediately tell you they also have a dog, but it is bigger, pedigreed, and comes from a long line of champions.

They tend to listen between the lines and pick up on everything that is said. Even if it is a benign statement or something said off the cuff, it is not uncommon for them to take issue with every comment someone else makes. Generally they will take the opposite point of view, whether they agree or not. If they do happen to agree, they will still find something critical to say or add an additional point as a form of one-upmanship.

Vocal Code

Competitors tend to be fast-talking and rarely let others get a word in edgewise. You usually hear tension in the voice; you may hear a twinge of jealousy.

Body Language Code

You will often notice a rigidity and a tension in competitors' bodies that indicates they are jealous. They often maintain a physical distance from those with whom they compete. Psychologically they do not wish to bond, so they rarely lean in when conversing.

On the other hand, they may force themselves to bond in order to get information. In that case, there may be an effusive amount of back slapping, handshaking, or hugging as a means of compensation for the fact they may be harboring some hostile feelings. Even though they may be carrying on with all of these seemingly endearing gestures, the tension and rigidity in their body movements indicate they are feeling jealous and competitive. Handshakes tend to be hard, hinting that they subconsciously want to hurt you.

They may fidget and move around since they are truly uncomfortable in your presence. They may also touch a great deal as an attempt to show dominance, or cover their chests when they speak—an indication they feel threatened.

When they speak, you may observe they've made a clenched fist. This may be an attempt to hide their true competitive and envious feelings.

Facial Code

Competitors' eyes generally dart around the room because it is uncomfortable for them to maintain genuine eye contact. They will sneak glances as they seek to maintain an edge.

They often gulp or lick their lips if they perceive you have some sort of an edge. You can expect to see these facial movements immediately after you have delivered some good news about yourself. They are not happy for you—deep down they are jealous and envious; as Freud said, they are seeking to destroy you.

10. The Giver

Speech Code

Givers are verbally open and highly expressive and communicative. They tend to speak in emotional terms about how people and certain situations make them feel. They tell you when they are feeling happy, sad, angry, if they doubt someone, or if they love someone. When they speak, they give a lot of themselves by revealing their true feelings. They have the ability to bring the focus of a conversation back to the other person and their experiences. They are more concerned about being interested in others than being interesting to others. They are unselfish, caring people.

They are sensitive in responding to your questions and concerns. They are generous and take their time explaining things and often give helpful information.

Givers are excellent listeners and rarely sing their own praises. They tend to be self-effacing so it is often difficult for them to accept compliments.

They say kind things out of a desire to give and to please others. They are very encouraging and motivating and would never dream of saying anything rude or hurtful. If they can't say something positive and helpful, they will usually say nothing.

Vocal Code

A giver's voice tends to be agreeable and pleasant. There is an upbeat, warm, and sensitive quality to the tone. The voice is often soft, mellifluous, and soothing.

Body Language Code

Givers tend to touch a lot and the touch is firm and direct. They usually have a warm, solid grip when shaking hands. They often use a double-handed clasped handshake, putting one hand over the person's hand as they shake. This makes others feel welcome. Givers tend to lean forward when they speak and listen, indicating their respect toward others.

They tend to be somewhat tentative and noninvasive in their body language and posture as they try to make themselves inconspicuous via their walk and stance. They may be slightly hunched over and may even walk softly, perhaps on their tiptoes, as they enter a room.

Facial Code

Givers have great eye contact and will always look directly at you. They often have expressions of compassion and concern and their eyes show both sympathy and empathy. They usually have a pleasant smile and appear to be approachable.

11. The Bully

Speech Code

Bullies are out to attack others at every turn with their hostile words. You will rarely hear anything good as they trash others behind their backs or to their face. Quick with a cutting remark, a backhanded comment, or sarcastic quip, their aim is to tear others down. Verbally belligerent and always ready for verbal warfare, they will dismiss others or cut them to shreds with their tongue. If you don't do things their way, you can be sure there will be turmoil on the horizon. In conversation, they usually discuss how they got the last laugh or showed another person a thing or two.

They are quick to tell you how to run your life and will give you their unsolicited opinion whether they know you or not. Self-righteous, stubborn, and rigid, they rarely compromise, apologize, or admit they were wrong. Even when they have clearly made a mistake, they always find someone else to blame and never shoulder responsibility for what they did.

They tend to speak in negative and hostile terms and curse words are second nature to them. They also tend to speak in absolutes and gross generalizations. They are inclined to be blunt and undiplomatic and can cut you down quickly. They also interrupt others in their attempts to control the conversation.

These people are accusers. Similar to the victim, they have a tendency to nag, instigate, and not let up as they bully you into doing something you didn't want to do. Although they can bully others with ease, they often cannot take it if they are bullied back.

Vocal Code

Bullies have a loud, alarmist quality to the voice, as if there is always impending danger. Their attacking tone often indicates they have a chip on their shoulder and reveals their inner hostility and anger toward themselves and others. Their vocal attempts to intimidate can be heard in the rapid, clipped, staccato tones that make them sound brash and aggressive.

Body Language Code

Bullies are not gentle; and they have a strong touch and a hard handshake. They tend to bulldoze everything in their path. They have a heavy gait and often make noise when they walk. Their forward-lunging posture demonstrates their aggressiveness.

Facial Code

Bullies usually furrow the brow when speaking. Their intense, penetrating, narrow gaze comes complete with flared nostrils and a hard stare, making for a tense expression.

As a rule, their lips are tight and pursed in rest position and they tend to speak in a closed-jaw fashion, indicating anger and hostility. They tend to thrust the lower jaw forward, a sign of aggression.

12. The Jokester

Speech Code

Jokesters are often the life of the party and people tend to gravitate toward them because of their quick wit and verbal acumen. Although they appear to view life as one big joke, they are extremely sensitive and usually have an overwhelming desire to be loved.

Because of this, and their perception that others are superior to them, they seek approval of others by verbally entertaining them.

They are free with compliments and quick comebacks. Their facile minds and myriad thoughts often result in fragmented speech as they flit from topic to topic, making them seem childlike. It may be difficult to follow them in conversation because they get side-tracked telling jokes and going off on tangents. Also like children, they tend to interrupt others in an attempt to get their points across.

Since jokesters need to be liked, they will say whatever it takes to make others feel good. They are free with compliments and usually say pleasant things to anyone.

Vocal Code

Jokesters usually speak in loud tones with a lot of bounce and exuberance. They laugh a lot and are gregarious and fun to be around. They talk constantly and may have a hoarse-sounding voice due to excessive and loud talking.

There is often a childlike excitement to the way they speak. They can make a mundane experience seem exciting by their effervescent and enthusiastic tones. They use a great deal of inflection and varied emotions and speak lively and rapidly, their words are easily deciphered.

Body Language Code

Jokesters seem to be in perpetual motion. It is a Herculean task for them to sit still. They tend to be physically energetic and will often approach strangers to joke around with.

They tend to touch a lot and have a need to be touched in return. They appear to have difficulty communicating without touching in some way. Since they have little regard for the space and boundaries of others, their well-meaning and benign touching may get them into trouble, especially if they touch someone who does not wish to be touched.

Similarly, they may stand too close to others when it may not be appropriate. It is not unusual to see a person back up while a jokester is inching forward, making it difficult for the person whose space they are invading.

As they converse, they tend to lean their bodies into others, a sign that they like the person. The truth is they like everyone they meet. Unfortunately, not everyone wants to know them and their overly friendly behavior can lead to awkward moments.

Jokesters use their arms and hands a great deal to punctuate their animated communication. They also tend to take up a lot of room, spreading out their arms and stretching their legs out in front of them.

Facial Code

Even when they are not speaking their lips may be parted because they always seem to be on the verge of saying something or interrupting someone. They tend to take in many breaths when they speak so you often see their chests heaving, similar to a small child.

Their facial expression is highly animated, though they often don't maintain eye contact because they tend to look everywhere when they speak. They do manage to make excellent eye contact with those who appreciate them.

They don't usually focus on one person, especially if there are a lot of people around. If they do focus on a particular person it generally won't be for long since they are easily distracted. They are usually first to see who walked by or entered a room.

13. The Unconscious One

Speech Code

It is not uncommon to hear them speak in fragments that make no sense. They may have several thoughts and may not be able to communicate them effectively. That is why it is difficult to follow what they say and it is not uncommon for them to be misinterpreted. They tend to flit from idea to idea, topic to topic, usually making perfect sense only to themselves.

In addition, they may impulsively speak every thought that goes through their mind, editing very little, much like children. As a result, they may appear blunt and insensitive and may hurt a listener's feelings even though they mean no harm. They always seem to be putting their feet into their mouths, making faux pas after faux pas.

As people get to know these unconscious chatterboxes, they are viewed with humor and compassion, or simply ignored as an embarrassment. They may speak too loud, or tell too much. When they do compliment someone, they are sincere and truthful. Sometimes they may be too truthful, using little discretion in what they say to whom.

They often leave their listener red-faced with embarrassment, as they will say anything, regardless of who's listening. They tell everything that's on their mind, talking to themselves or to anyone who will listen.

They lack social graces and verbal niceties. They may often use ethnic flavorings or slang during their conversation, regardless of whether anyone understands what they mean. They are poor listeners because they are so easily distracted by their own thoughts. They also dislike following directions as they prefer to do as they please.

Vocal Code

Unconscious ones are usually difficult to understand, mumbling in monotonous or overly emotional, inappropriately animated tones. Since they are often so preoccupied with their own thoughts, they tend to chatter to themselves. They may also sound nasal due to a failure to open their mouths to articulate properly. Their speech tends to drop off at the end of sentences, so it is difficult to understand what they say. Their rate of speech may also go to extremes—

too rapid or too slow, too loud or too soft. If they think of something funny, it is not unusual for them to laugh aloud, not sharing the joke with others.

Body Language Code

Their posture tends to be sloppy and it is not uncommon to see them walking around with shoulders slouched, head bowed, and stomach sticking out. They have a tendency to get too close, making others feel uncomfortable.

Unconscious people tend to gesture widely and awkwardly, using expansive arm movements and excessive hand movements and taking up an inappropriate amount of room. It is not uncommon to see them sitting with their feet underneath them or their legs crossed, Indian style.

Since these people are viewed as eccentric or preoccupied, they are often unaware of body odor, grooming, or personal cleanliness. They often lose things because they are so unconscious. They are a walking definition of "irresponsible."

Facial Code

Because of their tendency to be preoccupied with their own thoughts, they may appear to have a faraway gaze. They have poor eye contact and may not look at the person to whom they are speaking.

They pay little attention to appearances. It is not uncommon to find them with spittle at the corners of their mouths or on their lips when they speak.

14. The Real Dealer

Speech Code

Real dealers are verbally generous and speak with politeness and endearment. They think before they speak and rarely commit a faux pas. They are loyal and conscious about what they say and do. They are generous and sincere with compliments. They tend to speak positively and see the brighter side of life. They are people of their word who do exactly as they say and are not at all hypocritical.

They always realize they are responsible for the consequences of their actions and speak and act accordingly. They mean what they say and say what they mean. They accept people and don't judge. They are more interested in those around them than they are with themselves. Therefore, the focus of their conversation tends to be "outer" as opposed to "inner" directed. They share information and make sure there is genuine give-and-take during conversation.

Their communication is down to earth, humble, and unpretentious. They often possess a good sense of humor. They do not get laughs at the expense of others.

They are not sarcastic and would never think of verbally putting another person down. Real dealers are direct, get to the point, and are easily understood. They are excellent listeners who tend to draw out the best in others. They are appreciative and express their appreciation in a sincere manner.

Vocal Code

Real dealers use a wide range of emotion in their speech patterns. When they discuss something, they speak in tones that reflect emotion appropriate to the situation. If they are upset, happy, afraid, or unsure of something, you will hear it in their vocal tone. The pitch and the loudness of their voice vary depending on what they are discussing.

They have clear and intelligible articulation and the quality of their voice is deep, rich, and resonant. It sparkles with an enthusiasm toward life. There is a robust quality to the way they speak that makes people want to listen.

Body Language Code

They are loose and fluid in their body movements, which are inviting and make others feel comfortable. They are not afraid to touch others and often lean toward others when they speak. They tend to nod their heads in order to provide others with encouragement and to indicate their interest. Although they have a relaxed and comfortable posture, it is also strong, with the head erect, shoulders back, and spine straight.

They gesture grandly and enjoy hugging and touching. They effectively use their arms and hands to show interest and express certain points. When they gesture, the palms of their hands are often exposed with fingers extended, indicating they have nothing to hide.

Their legs are apart when they sit or crossed at the knees, as further indication of their openness. Feet are planted firmly on the ground, and they face the direction of the person with whom they are speaking, reflecting their sincerity.

Facial Code

Real dealers have excellent eye contact and employ a steady gaze. They make others feel as though they are the most important people in the world.

Their expression is normally relaxed and open, indicating they are receptive. They have fluid facial movements, a relaxed jaw, and slight smile when both speaking and listening. When they smile, it is a genuine smile with the corners of the mouth turned up and the corners around their eyes crinkled, communicating joy and happiness.

They reflect a facial expression that matches their verbal expression. If they are upset, you will not only hear the tone, you will see it in the face as well. If they like a person, their pupils will enlarge and they will smile often.

———

By now you understand the importance of using the four communication codes—the speech, vocal, body language, and facial codes—in order to form a more accurate assessment of people's personalities.

Now that you have this newfound wisdom, you will be able to see others with a whole new pair of eyes and hear them with a whole new pair of ears. You will have more data about the person, so you will be better equipped to make the right decisions about them. These decisions in turn will affect how you treat them and whether or not these people will be a part of your life.

Your newfound understanding of personality types will influence how effectively you communicate with others. Your new insight will also allow you to make fewer mistakes in your judgment and in your relationships with others. You may begin to find yourself becoming more tolerant, treating them with more compassion than you did before.

CHAPTER 10

Understanding What
It's All About

When scientists first learned to use a powerful tool like the electron microscope, they could see things never before imagined. Like these scientists, when we become aware of new and powerful tools and their uses, we, too, can learn from new information we never knew existed.

Now we have an opportunity to take a closeup view of people we meet by microscopically examining speech, vocal, body language, and facial codes, and personality types. Such heightened awareness often leads to red flags in determining a person's nature, character, and emotional state.

When the specific information contained in each of these categories is examined in tandem, the information provides an accurate and comprehensive profile of emotional state and personality traits, as we have learned throughout this book.

The ancient Greeks and Romans were well aware of the importance of immediately determining who was friend or foe or *knowing before whom they stood.* The survival of their civilization depended upon it. Likewise, every major religious doctrine discusses this concept of knowing before whom one stands. In fact most of Confucius' teachings are based upon the knowingness and awareness of specific types of people and the effect their character can have on you. The Hebrew Talmud and the Moslem Koran both discuss the value of recognizing specific traits within people that can affect your interpersonal relationships.

Today, this inscription is present in most synagogues throughout the modern world as it was in ancient times. The message reminds worshipers that when they stand during their worship services, they must remember before whom they are standing and praying—God.

If we embrace these words and apply them to any person who enters our lives, we will be more conscious of who they are and what affect they may have on us. We must judge others carefully and objectively and then take that data and confront ourselves emotionally in order to examine the type of person with whom we are dealing. We need to determine if they are sincere or lying or whether they are the kind of person that belongs in our lives. We need to observe as much as we can so we can accurately decide what role if any they will play in our lives.

Integrating All Four Codes of Communication

Most of us are intrigued by the notion of reading people, but we tend to read others by relying only on one or two of the four communication codes—person's body language or facial expression. Unfortunately, when you rely on a single code of communication or even two codes, you cannot be sure you have made an accurate assessment of the person.

Until this book, there has never been a method that allows you to simultaneously read a person by examining all *four* communication codes at once. That is why I use four ways to look at human behavior and have come up with a profile to help categorize people's actions based on their personality types and emotional states. I have told you to look at people in terms of how they make you feel emotionally. Now you can learn to trust your instinct in making an assessment of others.

The more you practice reading people, the more you sharpen not only your emotional and physical tools, but your intellectual and spiritual tools. Your brain is working better because you are incorporating many aspects of your neurological and sensory armory. As a result, you will be able to reach the right decisions. You will be able to face anyone standing before you and make proper choices.

Trust Yourself to Make the Right Decisions

Voices don't lie. Faces don't lie. Bodies don't lie. What someone says and how they say it isn't a lie. Unfortunately, people lie to themselves.

But after reading this book and incorporating the tools, it is no longer necessary to lie to oneself. No one has to be naive or refuse to listen to their instincts as they walk blindfolded across the busy superhighway of life. Both are dangerous and unnecessary risks no one has to take any longer.

Armed with this powerful understanding, you can now experience stunning insights into people you encounter for the first time. This will allow you to have greater self-awareness, more empathy toward others, and more self-confidence socially and in the business world. Now you will know what is real and what isn't. You will know for certain what is the truth and what is a lie.

You are not going to like everyone, nor should you. As I pointed out in my book *Toxic People,* there are people who are indeed toxic to you and will make your life miserable. On the other hand, some are terrific and will enrich your life and bring you joy, as I pointed out in *Attracting Terrific People.*

Life is filled with choices. Instead of making the right choices and feeling exhilarated about these choices and knowing they are the right ones, most of us unfortunately end up in a state of unease and constant confusion. But now you don't have to because your inner radar will be able to tell you when you are in danger and when you're safe.

Once you have made a decision about a person you've read, it will be time to act upon that decision. Don't keep going back to someone if you have decided that person is out of your life. Follow your instincts and don't deal with the person. If you are forced to because they are part of your work or family situation, then always be sure to keep your eyes open.

Remember, what you see and what you hear is what you get. You can't make people into your vision of them or what you want them to be. People who spend a lifetime trying to change others rarely succeed.

Sometimes you know you shouldn't deal with someone because they may be toxic to you, but you do it anyway. Just know that being in a toxic relationship can cause not only ill feelings but sickness as well. When you realize someone can literally put your life in danger, it is much less difficult to say no to that toxic person. There is no question that your welfare comes first.

You have the power. Use this vital information to your advantage and move on to a richer, more productive, less stressed-out life.

Read Yourself

After reading this book, you may be asking yourself, now that I know how to read others, how can I read myself? It is best done when someone takes a candid videotape of you so you can objectively see how you are coming across to others.

I am lucky to be able to read myself objectively from time to time as I often appear on television, where I am asked to comment on the psychological implications of various news events. As I look at the tapes, I can objectively assess how I am coming across. I examine my posture, gestures, and facial expressions as well as what I am saying. This lets me know how effective I was in getting my points across in a credible manner. If there is something I do not like, I am able to analyze what I did and why I did it.

Unfortunately, most people do not have the luxury of viewing how they appear to others, so getting an accurate reading of yourself is difficult. The next best thing is to become aware of what you are doing at all times—to be *mindful.* Pretend you are observing yourself and the person with whom you are interacting. Examine how you are speaking and what you are saying. Try to be conscious of your facial expressions and body movements. Most important, observe other people's reactions toward you. Do they sit close or lean in or are they moving away? What is the facial reaction? Do they look at you? Do they react to you or ignore you? Do they like being around you and do they like what you say? When you see how you are coming across, that is the best way to read yourself.

Develop Insight

My intention in writing this book is to share information so that you may know the truth about others and can find richer relationships. This book is *not* designed to make you into a professional manipulator who seeks to capitalize on other people's biases, ignorance, and impressionability.

By taking the time to *stop, look,* and *listen* to everyone you meet, you will develop uncanny insights into knowing people. And when you have an important choice to make about a person, whether a new partner or a new employee, you will be able to access answers in an efficient and accurate manner.

Your ability to read others will become second nature to you. The information you glean about them can save you from a lifetime of potential grief, and can create a lifetime of happiness, good health, and satisfying relationships.

APPENDIX A

Recommended Reading

Barbara, Dominick. *Your Speech Reveals Your Personality.* Springfield, Ill.: Charles C. Thomas Publishers, 1970.

Baron, Renee, and Elizabeth Wagele. *The Enneagram Made Easy.* New York: Harper, 1994.

Birdwhistell, Raymond. *Kinesics and Context.* New York: Penguin Publishing, 1973.

Blum, Deborah. "Face It!" *Psychology Today,* September–October 1998, pp. 33–38.

Bolting, Kate. *Sex Appeal.* New York: St. Martin's Press, 1993.

Darby, Joohn K. *Speech Evaluation in Psychiatry.* New York: Grune and Stratton, 1981.

Davies, Rodney. *How to Read Faces.* Wellingborough, England: Thorsons Publishing Group, Aquarian Press, 1989.

Devito, Joseph A. *Human Communication.* New York: Longman Publishing, 1995.

Dimitrious, Jo Ellan, and Mark Mazzarella. *Reading People.* New York: Random House, 1998.

Eaton, William J., and Norman Kempster. "Senators Want Glaspie Issue Clarified." *Los Angeles Times,* 1990, Section A.

Ekman, Paul, and W. V. Friesen. *Unmasking the Face.* Englewood Cliffs, N.J.: Prentice-Hall, 1975.

Ekman, Paul. *Telling Lies: Cues to Deceipt in the Marketplace, Politics, and Marriage.* New York: W.W. Norton and Company, 1985.

Elgin, Suzette Hayden. *The Gentle Art of Verbal Self Defense.* New York: Dorset Press, 1980.

Faigin, Gary. *The Artist's Complete Guide to Facial Expression.* New York: Watson-Guptill Publications, 1990.

Fairbanks, Grant. *Voice and Articulation Drillbook.* New York: Harper and Row, 1937.

Fast, Julius. *Body Language.* New York: Pocket Books, 1970.

———. *Subtext: Making Body Language Work in the Workplace.* New York: Viking Penguin, 1991.

Freud, Sigmund. "Psychopathology of Everyday Life" (1901). In *The Complete Psychological Works,* vol. 6, James Strachey, tr. and ed. New York: W.W. Norton, 1976, p. 86.

Fulfer, Mac. *Amazing Face Reading.* Fort Worth, Tex.: Q Publishing Services, 1998.

George, Jean Craighead. *How to Talk to Your Cat.* New York: Warner Books, 1985.

———. *How to Talk to Your Dog.* New York: Warner Books, 1985.

Glass, Lillian. *Talk to Win: Six Steps to a Successful Vocal Image.* New York: Putnam Publishing, 1987.

———. *Say It Right: How to Talk in Any Social or Business Situation.* New York: Putnam Publishing, 1992.

———. *He Says, She Says: Closing the Communication Gap Between the Sexes.* New York: Putnam Publishing, 1994.

———. *Toxic People: 10 Ways of Dealing with People Who Make Your Life Miserable.* New York: St. Martin's Press, 1997.

———. *Attracting Terrific People: How to Find and Keep the People Who Bring Your Life Joy.* New York: St. Martin's Press, 1997.

———. *The Complete Idiot's Guide to Verbal Self Defense.* New York: Alpha Books, Macmillan Publishing, 1999.

————. *The Complete Idiot's Guide to Understanding Men and Women.* New York: Alpha Books, Macmillan Publishing, 2000.

Hall, Calvin. *A Primer of Freudian Psychology.* New York: New American Library, 1954.

Hall, Calvin S., and Vernon, J. Nordby. *A Primer of Jungian Psychology.* New York: Penguin, Mentor Books, 1973.

Hall, E. T. *The Silent Language.* New York: Doubleday, 1959.

Haviland, Lewis. *Handbook of Emotions.* New York: Guilford Press, 1993.

Hurley, Kathleen V., and Theodore E. Dobson. *What's My Type? Use the Ennegram System of 9 Personality Types.* New York: HarperCollins, 1991.

Ingram, Jay. *Talk, Talk, Talk.* New York: Anchor Books, Doubleday, 1994.

Keirsey and Marilyn Baters. *Please Understand Me: Character and Temperament Types.* Del Mar, Calif.: Prometheus Nemesis Book Company, 1984.

Keleman, Stanley. *Emotional Anatomy.* Berkeley, Calif.: Center Press, 1985.

Knapp, M. L. *Nonverbal Communication in Human Interaction,* 2d ed. Boston: Holt, Rhinehart and Winston, 1972.

Korem, Sam. *The Art of Profiling: Reading People Right the First Time.* Richardson, Tex.: International Focus Press, 1997.

Kroeger, Otto, and Janet M. Thuesen. *Type Talk: The 16 Personality Types That Determine How We Live, Love and Work.* New York: Dell, 1988.

Kurtz, Ron, and Hector Prestera. *The Body Reveals: How to Read Your Own Body.* San Francisco: HarperCollins, 1984.

Lewis, David. *The Secret Language of Success: Using Body Language to Get What You Want.* New York: Galahad Books, 1989.

Lieberman, David J. *Never Be Lied to Again.* New York: St. Martin's Press, 1998.

Lowen, Alexander. *The Language of the Body: Physical Dynamics of Character Structure.* New York: Macmillan Publishing Co., 1971.

Luelsdorff, P. A. "On Language and Schizophrenia." *Folia Phoniatrica* 34 (1982): 72–81.

Marsh, Peter. *Eye to Eye: How People Interact.* Topsfield, Mass.: Salem House Publishers, 1988.

Maslow, Abraham H. *Motivation and Personality.* New York: Harper and Row, 1970.

Mason, Jeffrey Moussaieff. *When Elephants Weep: The Emotional Lives of Animals.* New York: Dell Publishing Company, 1995.

Mehrabian, Albert A. *Nonverbal Communication.* Chicago: Aldine Atherton, 1972.

Meyers, Isabel Briggs, and Peter B. Meyers. *Gifts Differing.* Palo Alto, Calif.: Consulting Psychologists Press, 1980.

Montagu, Ashley. *Touching: The Human Significance of the Skin.* New York: Harper and Row, 1986.

Mornell, Pierre. *Hiring Smart! How to Predict Winners and Losers in the Incredibly Expensive People-Reading Game.* Berkeley, Calif.: Ten Speed Press, 1998.

Morris, Desmond. *Horsewatching.* New York: Crown Publishers, 1988.

———. *Body Talk: The Meaning of Human Gesture.* New York: Crown Trade Paperbacks, 1994.

———. *Dogwatching.* New York: Crown Publishers, 1996.

Morris, James A. *The Art of Conversation.* New York: Cornerstone Library, 1977.

Moyes, Patricia. *How to Talk to Your Cat.* New York: Henry Holt and Company, 1978.

Nirerenberg, Gerard I., and Henry H. Calero. *How to Read a Person Like a Book.* New York: Barnes and Noble Books, 1994.

Oldham, John M., and Lois B. Morris. *Personality Self-Portrait.* New York: Bantam Publishing, 1990.

Patterson, Francine. *Koko's Kitten.* New York: Scholastic, 1985.

Quilliam, Susan. *Sexual Body Talk: Understanding the Body Language of Attraction from First Glances to Sexual Happiness.* London, England: Eddison, Saad Edition, 1992.

Riso, Richard. *Discovering Your Personality: The New Enneagram Questionnaire.* Boston: Houghton Mifflin, 1995.

Ruesch, Jurgen, and Weldon Kees. *Non-Verbal Communication.* Los Angeles: Unversity of California Press, 1974.

Steele, R. Don. *Body Language Secrets: A Guide During Courtship and Dating.* Whittier, Calif.: Steel Balls Press, 1997.

Tieger, Paul D., and Barbara Barron Tieger. *The Art of Speed Reading People.* Boston: Little Brown Company, 1998.

Wainright, Gordon R. *Body Language*. Chicago: NTC Publishing Group, 1985.

Wyllie, Timothy. *Dolphins, ETs, and Angels*. Santa Fe: Bear & Company, 1984.

———. *Dolphins, Telepathy, and Underwater Birthing*. Sante Fe: Bear & Company, 1993.

Young, Lailan. *The Naked Face: The Essential Guide to Reading Faces*. New York: Random House, 1993.

Zebrowitz, Leslie A. *Reading Faces*. New York: Westview Press, Harper-Collins, 1977.

Zunin, Leonard, and Natalie Zunin. *Contact: The First Four Minutes*. New York: Ballantine Books, 1972.

Gallup Poll Results Concerning Annoying Speech Habits

	TOTALLY ANNOYED	DOES NOT ANNOY	DON'T KNOW
Interrupting while others are talking	88%	11%	1%
Swearing or using curse words	84%	15%	1%
Mumbling or talking too softly	80%	20%	0%
Talking too loudly	73%	26%	1%
Speaking in a monotonous, boring voice	73%	26%	1%
Using filler words such as "and um," "like um," and "you know"	69%	29%	2%
Speaking in a nasal whine	67%	29%	4%

Talking too fast	66%	34%	0%
Using poor grammar or mispronouncing words	63%	36%	1%
Having a high-pitched voice	61%	37%	2%
Having a foreign accent or a regional dialect	24%	75%	1%

Index

Where to Get Additional Information
for Dr. Lillian Glass's Products and Services

Check out our website at: www.drlillianglass.com
E-mail us at: info@drlillianglass.com
Phone us at: (212) 946-5729
Write us at: Dr. Lillian Glass
P.O. Box 972
New York, NY 10021

Please fill out this form and mail to the above address. We will send you additional information.

Name:_____

Address:_____

City, State, Zip:_____

Phone:_____

Fax:_____

E-mail address:_____

Check areas you wish to receive more information about.

____ Other books by Dr. Lillian Glass   ____ Corporate training sessions
____ Audiotapes by Dr. Lillian Glass   ____ Private sessions (NYC) __ (LA) __
____ Videotapes by Dr. Lillian Glass   ____ E-mail consultations
____ *He Says She Says* greeting cards   ____ Telephone consultations
____ Music/CDs by Dr. Lillian Glass   ____ Audiotape consultations
      (*Emotional Healing /*   ____ Media consulting and training
      Mending Hearts)   ____ Newsletter
____ Seminars and lectures in your   ____ Other
      city or state